The Project

About the Author

David Power was born in Cork, Ireland. He studied Finance, Computing and Enterprise through Irish at Dublin City University and completed his MBA at INSEAD in Fontainebleau, France. In the last twenty years he has lived and worked in Ireland, Austria, Nigeria, India, New York, Singapore and Switzerland, mostly managing global multi-million-dollar projects for top-tier banks. He currently lives with his wife and two children in Zürich, Switzerland.

THE PROJECT

*Developing a Career in
Global Project Management*

David J. Power

ORPEN PRESS

Published by
Orpen Press
Lonsdale House
Avoca Avenue
Blackrock
Co. Dublin
Ireland

e-mail: info@orpenpress.com
www.orpenpress.com

Paperback ISBN 978-1-909895-50-8
ePub ISBN 978-1-909895-51-5
Kindle ISBN 978-1-909895-52-2
PDF ISBN 978-1-909895-53-9

Printed in Dublin by SPRINT-print Ltd.

Contents

1

What Is Project Management?

Getting fired is never pleasant. This was Colin's second time, so one could argue that he should have been used to it, but it doesn't work that way. At thirty years old Colin had never lived through a time when a job for life was the norm; instead he had experienced what seemed like a new norm of boom and bust. Maybe it was just that the cycles seemed shorter. He had experienced firsthand the dot-bomb that had followed the glory days of dot-com, when he was fired in New York. Now it was his turn to taste the financial crisis that has touched everyone in some way since. Colin's phone rang on Friday 11 September 2009 at one o'clock in the afternoon, almost exactly a year after Lehman Brothers filed for bankruptcy.

'Hello, Colin speaking.'

'Colin, could you join me for a discussion in Room 104?' John Newton, Colin's boss for the last two years, spoke in a voice without expression, as if reading a script. He paused. 'I'm here now.'

It was cold. The weather was to blame. The rains of the northeast monsoon that would usually begin to cool Singapore around this time had not yet begun and temperatures had hit record highs. Had Colin worked in the front office at Asia Corporate Bank (ACB), in the plush offices of the financial district, maybe the air conditioning could have handled the fluctuations. In the older, more industrial building on Bras Basah Road that housed the bank's Shared Services, the air conditioning was overcompensating. The Shared Services of ACB included IT, back office operations, HR and of course Finance, where he worked, specifically in Finance Change. He put on his suit jacket. He was dressed for the occasion. He felt cold.

Of course few people get 'fired' these days – except on reality TV – and that last time, in New York, he had been 'made redundant', during a 'downsizing exercise'. The meeting took place, he was given appropriate terms and that day he went home thinking he had no job. He spent weeks fruitlessly and despondently looking for a new one. He had in a way gone through this before. He had experienced that special feeling of one minute sitting on Connelly leather, in an open-top sports car, on an open road, with the roof down, on a sunny day and the next lying broken and in pain in a muddy and bloody ditch, having been hit side on by a truck and wondering how it could have happened. In the end Knowtec got its act together and technically it never happened. As was common then, while the US office was in crisis because it had too many staff, the Asia office was in difficulty because it did not have enough. The redundancy papers were torn up, the transfer papers finalised and Colin and his wife, Clara, landed in Singapore in time to experience the tail end of the SARS virus outbreak.

He knocked and opened the door. Room 104 was in a new annexe and the bright LED lights shining through chrome were reflected in the polished veneer of a long table. John was sitting at the far end with the HR person. Years later Colin could not remember what the person looked like. He was not there for his looks or his personality. He may not have even had one. He was there to represent a function and repeat verbatim what every other HR person would say in such a situation. He displayed no human emotion, no character or idiosyncrasy, no indication that he was living or dead. Colin imagined the reverse metamorphosis that makes a man an administrative function, a living synecdoche, an embodiment of HR.

'Colin, as you know, the banking industry as a whole is going through a difficult period.' John began reading directly from a typed page. 'A business review has been undertaken at ACB focusing on cost and the bank has begun a reduction in force exercise.'

Ah, so this time it would be 'reduction in force', Colin thought, suppressing the urge to smile. Being RIF'd was pretty new then, but later it would become passé and then the euphemism would become a derogatory and offensive term. He was thinking about this new buzzword because the rest felt too unreal to comprehend. People talk about spiritual out-of-body experiences but he truly was looking at the whole procedure from the outside. He saw, as if from a parapet high above, the bare windowless room with the stiff and silent HR person and John reading the script; and while he would have liked to say with bravado that he felt nothing, a slow sinking feeling haunted the shadows of his subconscious. He shivered and wondered if the same air conditioning fed the new annexe.

'This exercise is difficult for all staff, but, Colin,' John raised his eyes from the paper and allowed them to meet Colin's, 'unfortunately your role has been impacted by the review and today I am communicating termination of your employment with the bank.' Looking back at his script, he continued, 'HR will take you through the terms of your release from employment with ACB but if you have any questions for me now I will do my best to answer them. Do you have any questions?'

Who had chosen the green carpet tiles? Was there a whole department of carpet tile selectors? Would it be called Interior

Solutions Management? Would they be RIF'd today too? Did the sharp synthetic smell of newness come from the floor or the furniture? Could the aircon be colder?

'No, John, thank you.'

It was meant sincerely, and John knew it. HR, however, looked confused and, terrified of any possibility of diverting from the script, launched into the terms. Colin tuned out. He had seen them already. The thank you to John was for two years of support and mentorship as well as months of advance warning of today's main event. There were no surprises, but despite the absence of surprise, his full advance knowledge of the meeting and his sincere belief that the outcome was a good result, Colin was gutted. His position had been eliminated. Not only was he no longer wanted, his role was not required. Was it needed before? Had he been doing anything worthwhile? He knew that what he had heard was a script – not metaphorically, but an actual written HR-approved script that was read to everybody on the list. It was not personal. He knew this but it didn't help. He'd experienced this feeling before in what he viewed now as a test run, but this time it was real. After six years in Singapore and five at ACB he would have to start again.

'Now, as you do not have access to customer data or confidential competitive information', the HR man went on in that firm but practised friendly way only HR personnel have mastered, 'you are free to use company facilities for the next thirty days to assist your job search. Following this period placement services will be made available to you to provide external assistance.'

While happy with the services provided Colin could not help but feel slightly demeaned by the inference that he was not important enough to be escorted by security to the door, but he'd get over this. Closing the door behind him as he left, he fancifully compared the sound of wood against the rubber seal to a hardback cover closing against the last page.

He pondered whether this particular book was *Ulysses* or *Animal Farm*.

'Come on!' said John a few hours later as he and Colin discussed the morning's events without Big Brother looking over their shoulders, 'You're making out like a bandit!'

Colin could not disagree. His redundancy payment would be on more generous terms than was statutory in Singapore; and he would have a period of gardening leave, during which he would have access to the company's facilities. He had spent the day applying online to open roles in other banks while all the time subconsciously turning things over and over in his mind. Should he have been disloyal to John? Should he have fawned over John's replacement (a man who seemed to revel in obsequiousness), as he saw some of his colleagues do? Was he actually better off?

'What I don't get, though, is the short-term view. This time last year ACB agreed to fund my Masters in Finance and got me to sign a clause that I would have to repay the funding if I left the bank, and now they're pushing me out the door.'

John pulled out a chair and sat down. Colin's desk area was larger than the standard cubicle, with a higher partition and a small round table for meetings. It came with the title. It was not quite an office, but it was nonetheless a status symbol. It may have been ridiculous, but there were a hundred people on the other side of the partition who would gladly type the tops off their fingers just to sit in his seat.

'What you are missing is that a bank does not have a conscience that is continuous. Our new friend would probably disagree with the logic of the first decision to pay for your education and would now see it as a sunken cost unrelated to his reduction targets. It makes little sense seen holistically, but to each of the decision makers in the moment it is all perfectly sensible.'

Colin was unsure if he agreed. While probably true for practical purposes, that continuous conscience was probably the most succinct definition of company culture he had heard. If it's in a company's culture to invest in people for the long term it seemed wholly inconsistent to cut them for short-term targets. Either way Colin knew it changed nothing.

'What did you think about the bit about the industry downturn and all of that?' John asked with a wry smile.

Colin slid on his chair over to the small table where John was sitting. 'It was pretty convenient for HR, a complete copout!'

Of course it was just an excuse. This cull had been on the cards for months and John had given him the blow-by-blow account of MD corporate politics as it happened. It was demoralising to see John go through it and for some time Colin watched as a neutral outsider. Only in the last month or so did he know that he would be going down with the ship. John's role had been carved up piece by piece and given to his future successor, 'our new friend' as he called him, preparing for John's eventual takeout. He'd heard John sell these new developments in public as affirmation of the concentration and effort required of him in focusing on his 'core' role. In private John had told him how he felt the vultures were circling; he couldn't have been more candid back then, but had not lost hope. Now he sounded bitter.

'Slice by slice they cut my role away and fed it to the vultures. They're taking what I have built, polishing it and repackaging it as their own. They will completely dismantle some of it and move away entirely from the agreed strategy', he said, with as much sadness as bitterness. It seemed personal, a 180-degree turnaround from the straight, pragmatic, logical and dispassionate John whom Colin had known.

'Do you think Sriram felt the same when you arrived?' Colin asked, with a hint of a cheeky smile. He couldn't help but feel John was going too far.

'That was different. We were completely transparent. I was hired to take his role, he knew it and was forewarned. He handed it over to me. Look what we have accomplished since then. This is completely different.'

'Come off it, John, we work in Change. We manage projects. We are hired to dismantle the brilliant systems, ideas, processes and structures of our colleagues who have gone before us and rebuild them again in a different way that is hopefully more suited to what is done today. Of course, in the process the new thing needs to be faster, more efficient, less costly to run, create more competitive advantage, be less risky, enable greater trading volumes, allow for increased revenues and so on and so forth, but in the end we are hired to change stuff and it will never stop. Thank God, for as long as it continues we will always have work.'

Colin paused for breath and as John silently looked at him he wondered if he had gone too far. Would he have spoken to his boss this way if John were to do his performance appraisal at the end of the year? Perhaps he would, but it still felt a little uncomfortable, if not precocious, preaching Project Management 101 to a man twenty years his senior who had seen it all before. And to be fair he knew that once John finished reading his script to all who had shown loyalty to him he would then have it read back to him by 'our new friend'.

'I fear all this has made you overly cynical', John finally retorted. 'While change is constant a project has a start, middle and an end. It is not a continuous cycle that goes on for ever. It is temporary. It should create something new, be that a new process, a way of automating something that was manual, a better system, a more efficient process or a more effective structure, for example. The outcome should be tangible and success should be measurable.'

'I don't disagree with any of that', Colin interrupted.

'But what you don't see', John continued, 'is that in all of this we put some of ourselves into it. If we did not believe in the purpose of the project and the benefits of the outcome, what would be the point? Taking the logic further, when someone comes along and puts a stop to the progress we are making in achieving this goal we can, and do, feel personal loss as the goal to which we were committed will no longer be achieved.'

Colin was for a moment at a loss for words. If he was sitting before a junior project manager he would have understood, but John had been in the business a long time. He could see that it was hitting him even harder and that he was taking it personally.

'John, I get that you're down and the way they've done this is not right, but there is a difference between being passionate about what you do and being tied passionately to the original plan. It's because we can stay dispassionate about an outcome that we are best positioned to continuously review what is being done and to call it the way it is when the business has moved in a different direction independent of the project. We are the ones who need to call a stop to a project if we see that the money is not being spent wisely, if the reason why it was originally started no longer makes as much sense or if we can see that it's destined to fail. The worst project managers are the ones who keep pushing forward with something as if their career depended on it – even if their job in that moment possibly does depend on it.'

Colin could see the orange glow of the setting sun reflecting in the windows of the building opposite. At this time back in Ireland the sun would have gone down hours ago, but here, so near the equator, the length of the day changed little from one end of the year to the next. Singapore had no seasons as he would have defined them, just hot and humid or hot and wet. He didn't miss the cold mornings or the early darkness of winter, but the surreal feeling of summer sunshine at 10 p.m. and cool, fresh air that carried the scents of salt, seaweed and fresh mackerel was a luxury not sold at Takashimaya. It was around half past seven and he wondered why he was still in the office when he no longer even had a job there. He had called Clara earlier and was wondering how she was feeling. It was easy to preach, but it's only human to want one's work to mean something and have a lasting effect. He wondered if his did, if it would.

'We're human, after all', he began before John interrupted.

'And man cannot live on bread alone. Are you ready for a beer?'

Colin really did not want to; he'd had enough of the day and was ready for it to end, but John had done a lot for him in the last two years. He had worked hard, but without John's support he felt he would not have gotten very far. Everything, he believed, was half work and half chance and he had been pretty lucky to get the support he had gotten from John in the last two years.

'Ouch!' Colin said as he put his right hand behind his back and reached up with it to his left shoulder, 'you've twisted my arm.'

They pushed through the revolving doors and hit a wall of humidity in the amber-lit street. Five years in Asia had still not numbed him to the absurdity of leaving the cold of the building to hit the warmth of the streets. He welcomed it now for the first time as he felt the moment of freedom, knowing he had left nothing behind that he needed to be concerned about. In banking, so-called 'business as usual', BAU or back-office roles had the advantage, at least at more junior levels, of being complete at the end of the day for that day. The trades executed are executed; trades cleared or settled are just that, and anything left open is for the next shift to deal with. Each day started anew with new but usually similar problems to resolve and the same processes to follow. In a project anything not done that day would carry over to the next, and no day was ever the same. Today was certainly different, but anything left to be planned, measured, risk assessed or delivered was now someone else's problem.

The pub was only a few minutes' walk away and had as much atmosphere as a drive-through takeaway, but it was small and dark and had beer.

'What is it you think we do?' John asked, wiping beer foam from his upper lip.

Colin had had enough. He wanted to leave the day behind. 'Come on, John, let's just leave it.'

'Humour me!'

'Fair enough', Colin began. 'We manage delivery of work that makes new or improved stuff – a new system or a better service, for example. It should be at least some kind of a result that's enough work to warrant a formal structure and way to govern it.'

John let out a guffaw and tried to compose himself as some beer went down the wrong way. 'Not exactly a PRINCE2 standard definition', he said, smiling, referring to one of the project management international standards.

'Well, I went the PMP route', Colin retorted, smiling at the geekiness of their conversation and raising his voice as the music had been turned up. The music had no consistency – one minute eighties rock, Guns N' Roses or Bon Jovi and the next Britney Spears or Boyzone.

'Well if that's all you learned, your Project Management Professional certificate isn't worth the paper it's written on', John went on. 'What we do is to make the work that's done in the back office cheaper or help the front make more money. That's it.'

Colin sighed. 'Fine; in general terms we do all of the above, building systems and processes, to produce a benefit, and in banking that means increasing profits by reducing cost or increasing revenue. If we worked in an engineering firm you might say that by building a bridge we just shorten a commuting distance to make a person's commute cheaper.'

'That's exactly how we are taught to look at it – directly in terms of benefit realisation. It comes down to dollars and cents, pounds and pence.'

'What you're forgetting is that we need to look at the tangible benefits and the intangible benefits: the quantitative – your dollars and cents; and the qualitative benefits – the fact that John Driver gets home to see his kids half an hour earlier and when we hear Golden Gate or Brooklyn we think of bridges.' He was shouting now, as the pub became fuller and noisier. 'It may not be beautiful, but when your new straight through accounting ledger, or my regulatory reporting system, is completed people working in the back office will spend less time doing repetitive jobs that feel pretty pointless and they will spend fewer weekends at the end of the month on reconciliations and manual entries to get things right. I think that's worth it alone. Oh, and if you want to bring back my own cynical self, there is also the fact that we're well compensated for what we do!'

'I'll drink to that', said John, smiling. He could see that Colin was getting tired of his wallowing in self-pity. He couldn't help but feel a little envious of Colin, who was in the middle of his career and at a level where there was interesting work to be found and he seemed to be actually enjoying it. Roles at his own level, he knew, were more difficult to come by and were often filled by people climbing the ranks within a company. While he wasn't so sure about his own next steps, he knew Colin would have no problem moving on.

2

How to Interview for a
Project Management Role

The silence had been only intermittently broken by the
melodic lilting voice of the receptionist. A faint digital ring
followed immediately by 'Bank Investissement Belgique.
Good morning.'

Every time the answer was a pitch-perfect clone of the
time before, each of the eight syllables of the name carefully
enunciated in the chorus of her day. Just as the phrase and
accompanying melody began to repeat in Colin's mind, like
an earworm on the car radio, the roar of a landing jet betrayed
the proximity of the office to Changi Airport. He felt the
building shake. Had he been looking out of the window he
would have seen the giant before he heard the engines. When
he looked up and saw the monster descend he could see the
threading on the gigantic tires. He looked at the receptionist,
who seemed not to notice the shiny monster, but sensing his
gaze she looked up.

'They will be with you in just a moment. Are you sure you
would not like a drink while you are waiting?'

'Quite sure, thank you', Colin replied.

'Oh, excuse me. Bank Investissement Belgique. Good
morning.'

Colin reverted to gazing out of the window. He was as prepared as he could be for the interview: he had researched the bank online to get an overview, spoken to anyone he knew who worked or had worked there, researched the subject matter of the project for which he would interview and thought about his own resumé in the context of the job specification provided. Anything else, he felt, had to come directly from his experience, and that couldn't be prepared for; in fact, he believed, spontaneity based on direct honest answers came across far better in an interview. Instead of trying to relax before an interview, he would build in his mind the importance of the interview, how much he wanted the position and how suited he was for the role. He believed that this reinforcement of the goal and visualisation of the outcome would help his subconscious direct every answer to his desired outcome. Strongly internalising the belief would make every positive reaction quicker, truer and more believable. While imperceptible to the conscious mind, and a waste of time for logical decision-making, such nuances were in his view the building blocks of what directed the gut. He believed more than anything that an interview was not a time for deliberation or hesitation. There would be plenty of time for that later. As he focused, he could feel the flow of adrenalin that would help him think and react quicker. He listened to his own breathing, allowing long deep breaths to fill his lungs. The door to the office opened and a tall woman walked towards him and stretched out her hand.

'Hello, you must be Colin; I'm Helena Biel.'

'Hello, Helena', replied Colin, mirroring and matching her formality and tone. 'Thank you for taking the time to meet with me. I understand from Vikki Chong that you are here in Singapore for just a few days.'

'That's right', said Helena as she led Colin to the interview room. 'I flew in on Tuesday and I fly back tonight. I prefer to be home for the weekend. If I fly tonight I should be home early Saturday morning. The programme is pretty global – as head of change for BIB I'm based in Brussels. I say "home" as I have been based there now for more than ten years, though I'm originally from Switzerland. The project sponsor and some of the user group are based here and most of the IT department responsible for delivery is based in New York.'

Colin knew much of this from his pre-interview background research. It did concern him, however, as the time difference between Singapore and New York could not be more difficult to manage from Singapore. It could mean pretty late nights on conference calls and regular travel.

Though Helena was Swiss she spoke English with an almost unnatural perfection and a slight English accent. Colin felt himself subconsciously trying to guess her age and regained his focus before coming to a conclusion. He guessed later, when giving Clara the rundown, that she must have been somewhere between forty and fifty, but he could not be more precise. Her suit, while conservative and understated, was sharp and fitted and unquestionably professional.

The room was clean, somewhat grey and functional, with the bank's propaganda framed in glass on the wall. Wholesome, stylishly dressed people with white teeth and good skin looking with satisfaction at a chart climbing steadily from bottom left to top right. 'Bank Investissement Belgique, taking you where you want to go.'

'I appreciate you coming out here today. Was the office difficult for you to find?' Helena asked as she sat opposite Colin. It was a pretty standard opener, but Helena seemed genuinely interested.

'Not at all', replied Colin. 'In fact, I live quite close to this office on the east coast. Had we met in the city I would have had further to travel.'

While the small talk continued for less than five minutes it felt like much longer to Colin. He was impatient and did not want to be disarmed, did not want to be put completely at ease.

'That's nice. You have been in Singapore quite a while. You must like it here?'

'Yes, we have been here quite a while. It's a very comfortable lifestyle, though the time zone is not ideal from a career perspective.'

'Yes, I do agree with that; we have seen some of that in projects here where the hours can be somewhat extended when one is running a global book of work. Do you see yourself as being settled here, or do you think you will go back to Europe at some stage?'

Helena continued for a little longer, asking more about Singapore, his connections back in Europe and how he had ended up living in Asia. She then offered him a glass of water, which he again declined.

'So', Helena continued, with the subtlest change in her tone and posture, 'today, as you know, you are in for a bit of a marathon. Besides interviewing with me as hiring manager, you will meet with four other interviewers. Mike Gretchen, the sponsor, who as head of collateral commissioned the project, will speak with you as soon as we have finished. Roberto Giovanni, head of collateral IT, and his deputy, Serge Baranov, will then interview you together, and, finally, Vikki Chong from HR will conduct a competency-based interview.'

'Thanks, Helena, it's great that everyone is in the same place so I can meet so many people on the same day.'

'In my mind the role has three important considerations. We need someone who can lead a team to successfully deliver a project, have a high level of structure with consistent delivery methodology and understand the business processes to be implemented. The interview questions will be structured for the most part to help us understand if you can fulfil these considerations. I am sure our IT colleagues will also focus a little more on your ability to understand and work with technology. While answering the questions, I would appreciate it if you could focus on what you have done in the past, providing concrete actual examples. If you have not experienced what I am asking, it is best just to say so. I'll know anyway!'

Helena smiled as she said this, as if she was telling a little joke, but Colin was left in no doubt that she would see though any attempt to avoid a straight answer. He was surprised at Helena's openness. She was being explicit about what she wanted. Many times in the past he had spent half the interview trying to figure out what the interviewer wanted. In this case Helena was happy to tell her candidates exactly what was being looked for and ask them to prove they had it.

'Colin, during the interview I will also be taking notes, so I will occasionally lose eye contact. This does not mean I am not listening and I'd ask you to continue with your answer. Unless you have any questions, we can start.'

'It's clear, thank you', replied Colin, happy to finally begin in earnest. It had been eight weeks since John Newton had read his script at ACB and this was only the third company to grant him an interview, though he had applied for at least twenty positions. The market was even worse than he expected. His last interview was for a more junior position with a Swiss bank and after the fifth interview he was turned down. Without a visa-sponsoring company he would have to leave Singapore pretty quickly, but where would he go? Back to Dublin, or Munich, Clara's home town?

'Could you tell me what you know about the position?'

'As I understand it, you are looking for a project manager to lead a project that has already been running for a full year in the area of collateral.'

'I see by your CV that you have some relevant project management experience that I would like to cover in more depth, but before we do that I would like to get a feeling for your understanding of the business processes. What do you know about collateral management?'

'I'm no expert', replied Colin, as confidently as if he had worked in collateral processing all his life, 'but simply put, it is a way of securing a transaction and reducing credit risk associated with the potential for default. Collateral can be pledged up front as initial margin and other times collateral only needs to be exchanged when the value of an underlying security changes, for example when a stock price changes. If collateral is exchanged and can be reused it is called rehypothecable. I could go on, but as you ask me more and more questions you will find that what I know is what I have studied before the interview and not what I have gained through experience of working in the area. As I said, I'm no expert, but that will not impact my delivery capabilities. Do you believe a project manager needs to be an expert in the subject matter of the function in which the project is being delivered?'

Helena paused for a moment and Colin wondered if he'd gone just a little too far, too early, in pushing the question back to her, but Helena was considering her response. It was a controversial debate. She had her own views, but she knew that business stakeholders in the project had less respect for people who did not know their business as well as they did. They questioned how those without the same detailed understanding could lead change. She paused as she remembered the discussion she'd had with Mike Gretchen only thirty minutes before the interview. While she needed little convincing, she needed to play devil's advocate while ensuring that the business stakeholders could accept Colin. If he could not be convincing to the wider group he would be set up for failure.

'Some would say that without a detailed understanding of the processes to be changed a project manager cannot implement the changes necessary to make them better. What would you say to those people?'

'I agree that a project manager needs to understand the business processes within a project', Colin replied, using the same words as Helena had used five minutes earlier in describing the interview structure. 'I believe, though, that if a project manager understands the basics and if he is reasonably intelligent he can pick up what is necessary to maintain respect in the business while learning more as the project progresses. I know in an interview it's difficult to gauge whether a project manager will be able to work in this way, but I believe that if it can be evidenced by experience this should give any reassurance that might be necessary.'

Helena was warming to Colin – he was giving her the answers she was looking for – but was wary of her own eagerness to fill the role. Getting a warm body of any type would give her immediate relief from the hands-on management she had been forced to do after stepping in when the last manager resigned. She was conscious, however, that selecting the wrong candidate would mean more grief just a little down the line. She knew she needed to push harder and took his bait.

'And of course you can evidence this?'

'As you can see from my CV, I started running projects in ecommerce, implementing systems that allowed banks to move less complex foreign exchange and money market trades away from the trading desk to online portals. When I did this I had subject matter expertise of online FX but I had little experience in running projects and I had to pick this up along the way. As I gained understanding of project management methodology I added other ecommerce projects, where I had less expertise, to my portfolio. When I moved departments I successfully delivered a programme that created a new reference data system for use across the bank, though I had no previous reference data experience. I then moved to the finance department and ran projects implementing a new accounting general ledger. I understood general accounting but had no real expertise there. I believe that to be successful we need at least one element of the three requirements you mentioned to be exceptionally strong if the others are not equal. In my first project management role it was my business expertise. Now it is my skills and experience as a project manager I can rely on while building up knowledge in the business area.'

Helena could see some of her own career progression in Colin's description. She wondered, however, how Colin could convince Mike Gretchen. His opinions were pretty strong, but it was out of her hands. They had interviewed two subject matter experts already but unfortunately neither of them could have managed themselves out of a paper bag. Even Mike recognised this but was still holding out for a collateral expert with structured project management experience who didn't want to build a career in collateral processing. Helena decided to leave her thoughts around Colin's competence to pick up the subject matter and focus on project management, which would be questioned less by the other interviewers. Even when it was obvious that the candidate had relevant experience, asking these questions gave her a feeling of what kind of project manager she was dealing with it. She had interviewed candidates at both extremes: while one project manager would do nothing unless it was to the letter of a particular structured methodology, another would manage to get by with little use of any tools and still get things done. Helena was looking for that middle ground, someone who knew the rules well enough to understand when breaking them would be most appropriate.

'Can you describe to me the triangle of project constraints?'

'It means that basically something's got to give', replied Colin. 'The theory states that quality is in the centre and project scope, time and cost on each of the sides, and if one moves it affects at least one of the others.'

'You say it's a theory, but do you see this in practice?' Helena continued, again allowing herself to be led.

'As long as we stick to saying something's got to give I am happy with the theory and it stands up in many cases. For example, if you expand project scope, this side of the triangle grows, then logically either the time it takes to deliver the project or the cost of the project, or both, will grow accordingly. If they don't, then you expect me to deliver the extras in the same time for the same cost and the quality, or triangle area, decreases as it is flattened. I could use the same example if you decrease my cost and leave the others the same. It's a nice illustration but in some cases it doesn't hold completely true, for example if money is thrown at a project in the wrong way sometimes it changes nothing but the run rate.'

Helena could feel the time ticking by; she was getting the right feeling from the interview, but it was important for her to feel that she had completed due diligence on the areas where she was expected to give an opinion. BIB was not a place where decisions were made alone. A collaborative approach was seen as generally good practice and giving this position to a new hire meant a lost opportunity to an internal candidate. While she knew from his experience and the way he was handling the interview that Colin could handle the job, he would be set up to fail if she pushed him through without the other stakeholders feeling they too were part of the decision to make the hire.

'This project is in flight, as you may know, but if it were to start afresh, how would you estimate how much it would cost and how long it would take to get a particular IT project done?'

'How long have I got to come back with an estimate?' Colin asked, knowing that this would make all the difference.

'You have an hour and the sponsor is waiting to take it to the board.'

Colin smiled. He wasn't sure he would want to work for a sponsor who would go into a board meeting half cocked with little data supporting a funding request.

'Given the timeframe, I would not have the luxury of seed money or time to do proper analysis; I could not look at the detailed scope and build estimates from the bottom up, getting indicative quotes from IT development teams. I would compare the project to projects I have run before and ask around in the organisation, in the project management group and in IT for the cost of similar projects that had been completed.'

Colin kicked himself later for not thinking of the term 'analogous estimating', but Helena seemed happy enough with the response.

'If you were to start tomorrow, what would you do?'

Colin was wary of the answer. It was a pretty subjective question as some interviewers would expect and prefer the focus to be on specific areas. Some interviewers would expect a week of reading the project documentation, for example the project initiation document or PID, the project plan, the business requirements focusing on scope, the business case for the reasons to do the project in the first place, the issues and risks logs to see what the problems of the project were perceived to be; or at least the latest status report. He decided to go in another direction, as it was how he had done things before.

'The first thing I would do is talk to people. I'd meet as many people as I could, starting with the project team and sponsor, then the IT teams and business representatives. I would gather their views on the basis for the project, how things are going, what they hoped the project would achieve. I would try to spend my first days listening. I would then move to a review of the main project documents, starting at a higher level and moving to a detailed level. I would ask the people who wrote the documentation to walk me through them, as that would allow me to build relationships as I build my own knowledge. Once completed I would then begin to assess where the project is in terms of structure and begin to make changes as necessary until I feel it is in control.'

'Would you follow a particular methodology in doing this?' Helena asked.

'If you mean would I follow PRINCE2, PMI or another structure, I believe, and I hope you won't think less of me for it, that they all preach a similar sort of religion. Unfortunately, like religion, some people have zealous beliefs that there can be only one way of doing things. I feel that they both preach a structure and logic that can be necessary given the right circumstances. If the bank follows a particular methodology I am quite happy to follow this; otherwise I would be structured in my approach, applying methodology and using project management tools where necessary. I believe in structure, but not just for the sake of it.'

Helena paused for a few moments, and looked at her notepad. She had written the word 'structure' with an exaggerated question mark beside it. She was a fan of methodology, there were solid subject matter experts in the group and delivery drivers, but the point of project management, she felt, was the structure itself, the framework within which delivery could be directed and transparency provided. For anything small she could trust any businessperson of reasonable calibre to get on and do things and even have some structure and transparency, but for more complex projects it was the ability to apply the project management toolkit that brought some value and justified the cost of the extra resource. It was also what the project needed. While she was glad Colin had not bored her to tears extolling the virtues of one methodology over another, she wondered if his answer was just that little bit too flippant. He would only have used the full set of tools had he run larger projects.

'Tell me about the biggest project you have managed', Helena asked at last.

'It all depends on how size is measured', replied Colin. The faintest glimmer of a smile flitted across Helena's face and the feeling he was on the right track gave Colin further confidence in his answer. He decided to leave budget as a definition until last.

'The general ledger implementation you see on my CV had fifty interfaces, the funds transfer pricing rollout was implemented in sixteen countries across four continents in six languages, the online FX system had one hundred thousand users, but it was the reporting system that cost the most at ten million dollars. Incidentally, this was the least complex as most of this money was paid directly to a vendor for the licence fees and some small modifications.'

'You mentioned not applying structure for the sake of it; were you able to manage these projects with a light-touch approach?'

'Unfortunately not', Colin replied. 'We needed to throw everything at some of these. The scope and requirements were tightly controlled. We observed tollgates between phases with entry and exit criteria, documentation was standardised and signed off at all phases, the plan was baselined and change control executed against it. As I mentioned earlier I don't believe in structure for the sake of it, but sometimes it is a necessity.'

Helena breathed a sigh of relief. She had allowed herself to be convinced early in the interview and had fought almost with herself to push Colin in the wrong direction because she needed to be sure that she could stand behind him. He had come through it and she was glad he had. While interviews seem long, living with a bad decision is an eternity in comparison.

'Colin, I have asked you everything I wanted to ask today. Do you have some questions you would like to ask me?'

The greatest advantage of back-to-back interviews, in Colin's opinion, was not saving travel time. If done correctly he believed that each interview could be leveraged to make the next one better. Things learned in the first could be played back as answers to questions in the second and subsequent interviews. It reminded him a little of the novice who played two chess masters simultaneously in different rooms. The novice took the opening move of the first master as her opening move against the second. She took the counter of the second master to counter the opening move of the first. Knowing only enough about the game to understand how to act as a conduit between the two masters, she played like a true master herself. Though he knew some might see this as deception, Colin saw it as leveraging expertise and part of project management itself. The ability to leverage information between interviews also showed aptitude, forward thinking and stakeholder management skills, in his mind, and this type of first-hand information could confirm or shatter a first impression.

'I was wondering how the sponsor would view the benefits of the project as described and how the project is intending to measure these.'

Helena answered as candidly as he had hoped.

'And besides needing a project manager, is the project delivering to schedule and cost for the original scope? What would you think are the greatest challenges?'

Again Helena was frank and forthright in her reply.

'A final question, if you don't mind, Helena.' Colin felt he was pushing the limits but took his chances. He knew from his own experience of being at the other side of the table that in answering questions at the end of an interview the interviewer can sometimes be more candid, as if they feel a need to reciprocate the process of giving information.

'Having interviewed me today, what would be your greatest concern in my ability to be successful in this role?'

Helena didn't even blink.

'There are two things that come to mind. First, every person has his or her own style. Your style and confident disposition will sit very well with some people, but assuming you are consistent and do not tailor your approach, it will not sit well with others. If you change and adapt your style according to the situation you will run into trust issues with your stakeholders, as they will not know who you are. The second is product knowledge – we discussed this earlier. I get it and I can support your approach, but others would take more convincing.'

And with that Helena stood up, and after thanking Colin for his time, and explaining that the next interviewer would come along shortly, she shook his hand and left the room.

Another aeroplane roared heavily overhead as it floated lightly towards the runway. Colin wondered if any had landed during the interview; he didn't remember any but couldn't help but feel that there must have been some landings. His world might have stood still, but life went on.

It was a good five minutes before Mike Gretchen arrived and Colin guessed that Helena had briefed him on the previous interview. He burst through the door with such force that Colin was thankful he had not stood up to stretch his legs, or he would surely have been knocked over by the velocity of the whirlwind that entered the room. Mike was tall, grey and imposing. Heavily built, strong even, and not perceptibly overweight, he moved like a man half his size. He wore a suit with a jacket, which Colin found a little unusual for Singapore. His shirt collar was at least a size too small and together with the large veins on his neck and his red face he looked as though his tie was about to strangle him. Before he opened his mouth Colin know that Mike would talk fast and guessed that the aura of haste he exuded was less a product of his day and more his innate personality. It felt as though Mike filled the room. After the briefest of introductions Mike launched straight into his questions, his intonation and attitude bordering on hostility.

'Look, Conor, I don't want to waste your time', he began, as Colin registered that he'd been called the wrong name and the fact that Mike really meant he didn't want to waste his own time. 'I've read your CV and I can't find the word 'collateral' in a single place. Could you help me understand why we are talking today?'

Colin smiled and took a single breath before answering. He felt that matching Mike's pace and tone would increase the tension and turn the interview into an argument rather than a discussion. He needed to take control and to de-escalate the situation while at the same time showing respect to Mike. He began confidently in a forthright tone with a fast pace that he began to slow down as he spoke.

'I appreciate your honesty. Before we go any further I want to clarify that my name is Colin – I may not have said it clearly as you took me by surprise when you entered the room. Now, as I understand it, the reasons why you commissioned this project are threefold. The process managed today lacks control, is inefficient and is not built into the trading process or pricing in any meaningful end-to-end way. To get this right you need a target operating model – a TOM – defined for collateral, including clear roles and responsibilities between the front office and processing areas, and you need it implemented in the most efficient and automated way.' Colin paused for a moment, saw that Mike was about to open his mouth, and continued more slowly and deliberately, and so quietly that Mike had to lean forward. 'You are talking to me today because this transformation process is my bread and butter. This is what I do', Colin said, emphasising each word of the last sentence as if he were spelling it out.

'Well, Colin', Mike retorted at the mere hint of a break in Colin's response, and over-emphasising his name, 'how can someone lead this level of change without understanding the process?'

'Mike, I'll have to correct you there; I do understand the process', Colin countered and launched into the collateral processing description that he had practically learned by heart. 'What you might be referring to, if you will excuse my interpretation, is my lack of understanding for your very own process in Bank IB operations that you manage. That is absolutely true, but then the only people who know this in any great depth are the people working with it today. While it might be bold to say it, I believe that if they have lived and breathed it they may feel protective of it and would not be as adept at changing it as someone with less skin in the game.'

'You've told me enough of the qualities that you see as your strengths. Tell me about your weaknesses and for goodness' sake don't tell me you're too detailed, too conscientious, that you find it difficult to manage your work–life balance because you work too hard or any of that guff, and give me a real example of where it hurt your delivery.'

'Fair enough, Mike. In the past I've been too focused on delivery itself and not enough on the people who make it happen. I'm not dressing up a quality as a weakness, because this is a contradiction in terms. It's the people who make the delivery happen. In the reference data project I ran we were working sixteen-hour days and I believed that if I could do this there was no reason why everyone else should not do the same. I had a fifty per cent staff turnover in two months and we missed our delivery because of the loss of project, systems and institution knowledge within the team. I've learned from this and I am more careful about team morale, about working together and about staying close to the ground. I try to get the team out of the office for a lunch or a drink. I don't need to be anyone's best buddy, but there should be solid working relationships in project teams.'

Mike did not respond. He had his head down and was drawing boxes and lines almost feverishly in his notebook with a stub of a pencil with an eraser head that had been half chewed off. He slapped the pencil with satisfaction on the notebook, swivelled the pad around and passed pencil and paper to Colin.

'Here, then! What's wrong with this and what would you do to change it?'

Colin looked in shock at the scribbled diagram. He was beginning to feel that there was something surreal about Mike's rudeness and aggression. He felt like he was trapped in an eighties police drama where the characters were hamming it up playing Good Cop, Bad Cop. He focused on the drawing.

'Well, before I try to change it let me understand it first. You've drawn what looks like a trade life cycle process. The trade gets booked in this system in the front and it looks like it is enriched here manually', he said, pointing to a stick man. 'There is a trade verification process, confirmation process, settlement and some reconciliations. Am I broadly right?'

'So what's wrong with it?'

'In my view it's too complicated and has too many manual touch points. The trade data and static data come from multiple systems, and there are no golden sources or trade repositories. There are too many points of reconciliation. In short, it's a mess.'

'And what would you do about it?'

'First, if you take the data from a golden source you can eliminate reconciliations here, here and here.' Colin drew circles with the pencil stub. 'The three systems here do settlement for different product types. Surely this could be consolidated and if you were to employ further automation these manual touch points could be reduced to increase efficiency and control', Colin said finally, searching in Mike's eyes for some kind of reaction. 'Am I warm?'

'It's good enough', Mike replied, at last allowing a thaw in his voice and posture. 'I'll let the others know they can come in a bit earlier.'

It had been less than fifteen minutes. Helena had given Colin a positive review but felt that she had not got very far under the surface. Mike told her that he would break him and he now felt he had completely failed in this regard. While he felt his ego deflate, he acknowledged that Colin was one of the better candidates he had met so far. He left, and Colin closed the door quietly behind him.

Scarcely a moment later there was a soft knock on the door and Roberto Giovanni, the head of collateral IT, and his deputy, Serge Baranov, entered the room.

'Hey, how are you doing?' Roberto began, as New York as De Niro, stretching out his hand across the table. 'I'm Roberto and this is Serge.'

Serge raised his eyebrows in acknowledgement and greeting and sat down. He looked like he would rather be somewhere else. Roberto, on the other hand, smiled broadly as if he knew something no one else did. His hair was too black for his age and the top three buttons on his shirt were open enough to display a gold chain. He sat low in the chair and hung his arm over the back. Serge sat bolt upright in his short-sleeved shirt as if ready to demonstrate posture at a 1920s finishing school. He had three pens of different colours arranged neatly in his shirt pocket and pen marks above the pocket from replacing them the wrong way round.

'We thought it would be good to meet with you while we are in town', Roberto continued. 'It's always good to have a sit-down face to face, don't you think?'

Colin was unsure for a moment whether it was a rhetorical question or if Roberto was looking for a response. He was about to answer when Serge interjected.

'I can see by your CV you worked on quite a few software delivery projects, some of them on the IT side and others working from the business side. What was the difference?'

'I think it all comes down to agreeing roles and responsibilities and focusing on relationships', Colin began, looking in turn at Serge and Roberto to ensure that he was talking to them both and maintaining eye contact. 'In some of the projects I managed IT delivery only and focused on IT coding, unit testing, quality assurance – QA – and systems integration testing – SIT. I would manage the defects and change requests that came from the user acceptance testing – UAT – and would ensure post-UAT that we had an effective go-live plan. When I worked for mature project organisations I would partner with the business project manager and, while we understood our own roles and responsibilities, we felt jointly accountable for delivery. In some organisations I played the role of business project manager and I also sometimes did both roles together.'

'What I think my friend Serge is asking', Roberto interrupted, still smiling, 'is what the difference is for you? What did you prefer and why? What did you not like so much?'

'I enjoyed the challenge of running both roles simultaneously but I enjoyed it most when IT and the business groups could work closely and in partnership. I probably have most fun when this works well. I dislike it when there are power struggles between the two groups and when people don't get on or point fingers when things go wrong.'

'Have you experienced this? And how did you deal with it?' Serge asked, almost without emotion, while Roberto still looked as if he was genuinely having a good time. Colin wondered if it was because this was a break from sitting in a room discussing project issues with Helena, Mike, Serge and who knows who else. Maybe it was Roberto who was getting the grilling there.

'Yes, and it's not enjoyable at all', Colin replied, trying to focus on the experience of working together. While Helena and Mike needed results, Serge and Roberto would want someone they could work with to get those results. 'There's nothing worse than arguments between groups on what is a defect versus a change request, what was coded to the letter of the specification and what was coded to the spirit of the requirement.'

'And what do you do then?' asked Roberto.

'Well, they say conflict avoidance is a poor way to deal with things', began Colin, ready to launch into one of his set pieces.

Interviews, he believed, are like English essays in a final exam. No matter what the topic, there should be some set pieces you feel you've got right that can be pulled out of the bag. Strengths and weaknesses should be set pieces, as should dealing with conflict, project life cycle, budgeting and many other standard questions. It was simply good preparation. There are different levels of experience on the interviewer side of the table as well, and while some interviewers – like Mike Gretchen – might throw a curve ball, they would still reach into the standard bag of questions because the old ones really are the good ones. How could anyone possibly hire a project manager without knowing how he or she manages plans, people, issues, risks, budgets and stakeholders? As with most things, there is a standard bell curve, and having good answers to the twenty questions in the belly of the curve is half the battle. There should be little thinking involved in the answer; instead, the thought process should go into tailoring the answer and how to give it in the moment. If the answer is a given, the brain has plenty of bandwidth to be creative.

'I believe, however, that if you can avoid conflict by preparation it will arise far less. Good relationships are the first place to start. If people are on good terms they are less likely to take offence. If I call my best friend an idiot he will take it to mean that I believe he's pretty smart but that in a particular instance we have a different opinion. If I call a person with whom I have no relationship an idiot he's going to punch me in the face.'

Roberto guffawed and Serge looked sideways at him in mock disapproval. Colin thought they would say something but they waited, expecting him to continue.

'Looking at things in these terms people can focus on the common goal of successful delivery, and a better bonus.'

'Ha!' blurted Roberto – more Al Pacino this time – as if there was a fat chance of that outcome.

'But you still have not answered the question', persisted Serge. 'When conflict does arise, with IT for example, if you are leading the project as the business project manager, how do you handle this?'

'In such cases I do not avoid conflict; in such cases I believe it needs to be handled head on, but in as collaborative and forward-looking a way as possible. Lessons learned can be agreed once a project has been delivered, but during the project it is about the best steps to move the project forward. So to answer your question, I would work with the IT team to resolve issues together, looking at the best outcome to help everyone be successful.'

Serge didn't look ecstatic, but then Colin wondered if he ever did. At least he didn't look unhappy with the answer.

'Do you think Java or Visual C++ should be used to code the product interfaces?' Roberto asked, as if he wanted to catch Colin by surprise.

Colin could see that Roberto's smile looked even cheekier than it had before and let himself become just a bit more familiar.

'Come on Roberto, you're playing with me, that's your job. I stick to the rules well enough, I let the business guys describe what they need in their requirements, we describe how that will be structured into functions of a system together and you build it however you need to satisfy those requirements. If it smells like you're building a Cadillac when a Chevy will do I would think we should be able to discuss this though.'

'Have you ever run a project that failed?' asked Serge.
Colin reached into his bag of answers again. This one was a stalwart damned-if-you-do damned-if-you-don't question. If you have never been part of a project that has failed at least partially, you have little experience. If you have run a project that has failed, then what does that say about you?

'I have run a project that failed miserably', began Colin, and even Serge looked as though he was going to smile. 'At ACB we poured ten million dollars into a project to create the best automated trading system for clients trading FX under one million a trade. The types of trades that required no dealer intervention, just automated pricing, execution and straight-through confirmation. We got the system live, but by the time we did the world had changed and such clients were only interested in trading on portals where they were provided multiple prices for the same request. While the project was a failure, as the client interest did not justify the spend, we did have a pricing engine that we could reuse to hook up to the portals, so in the end it was not a complete waste.'

'Thanks, Colin, it was good meeting you', Roberto said as he half got up and then sat down again. 'Do you have any questions for us?'

Colin glanced at Serge, who was looking at his watch.

'Thanks to both of you for taking time out of the onsite to talk to me. I don't think I have any further questions for now.'

Roberto and Serge got up and shook Colin's hand before leaving, and Colin felt Serge's handshake was like that of an opponent at the end of a tough game. If that was the case, though, he wasn't sure who had won. He breathed a sigh of relief. He was feeling tired and mentally drained. He closed his eyes for a moment and listened to the sound of the air conditioning.

'Is everything all right?'

It was Vikki Chong. Colin was almost surprised to see an Asian face. He wondered about the ratio of Asians to Europeans in the Singapore office and if that changed through the hierarchy.

'Yes, thank you. You must be Vikki', Colin replied as he got up to shake her hand.

'Yes, that's right, we spoke on the phone. How are things going?' she asked, looking a little concerned.

'It's been pretty intense, but I think it's going well. I've met a lot of the team and everyone seems very interested in the success of the project and that's always a positive sign.'

Vikki played an interesting role in that her job was to get people in the door and her short-term success depended on hiring. Her reputation and therefore her future success, on the other hand, were determined by the quality of the candidates she put forward and were hired. Colin was trying to read her, but she was not giving much away.

'Well the way we run the last interview is less an interview and more a written exercise, and you can take your own time, so you might feel a little less pressure.'

Vikki opened the bundle she was carrying and passed Colin some papers.

'These are what we call competency-based questions. I'm sure you are familiar with the format. Simply put, they are questions designed to allow you to tell us about times when you demonstrated qualities that we believe are important. The space for answers is pretty limited; we're not looking for a story, just succinct examples. I'll leave this with you and once you are done you can pop it in this envelope and hand it to Angela at reception. She will put it in the internal mail to me. Do you have any questions?'

And then Vikki was gone, no doubt to a different interview room to say similar things to another candidate for this or another role. Colin looked through the questions briefly. He had answered some of them orally in earlier interviews, some were standard enough, and a few were a little unexpected. An internet search for 'competency-based interview questions' could yield millions of results and while there was a bell curve, it was pretty flat with some long tails. 'Tell me about a time ... when you demonstrated good leadership skills ... when you faced a crisis and how you responded ... when you had to make a decision with less information that you thought necessary ... when your communication skills made a difference.' What worried him most were not the answers to the questions but his own handwriting and spelling.

3

First Day in a New Project Management Role

'Bank Investissement Belgique. Good morning.'

Having heard it so many times when last he sat in reception preparing himself psychologically for the interview, Colin welcomed the receptionist's patter as a homely, familiar sound. Tone and enunciation were still pitch perfect. 'Consistency in a world gone mad', he thought. He was met in reception by Jason, who it turned out was the delivery lead on the processing stream for over-the-counter or OTC trades, the type that are not listed on any exchange.

It had only struck him once he had accepted the job offer that during the interview he had asked questions he felt would help him get the job, but not those he would care about on the first day. What kind of a team is in place? How is the programme structured? Are there any sub-project or delivery leads in place? How is team morale? Is there high or low staff turnover? Why did the previous project manager leave, or was he fired? Besides needing a new project manager, is the team complete? Does it have enough business analysts? Is there a testing team in place? Are there sufficient subject matter experts (SMEs) in place? He dismissed any regret at this realisation and held firm to the belief that only questions that would move the interview forward were appropriate in the interview itself. If there were questions that needed to be answered before he accepted the position he could have asked them after the offer was made, but he didn't think that the answers to any of these would have made him reconsider. All other questions could be answered in good time.

'Welcome Colin, I'm Jason Tan. It's great to have you on board', Jason said as he shook Colin's hand.

'Good to meet you too, Jason; I'm glad to be here', Colin replied genuinely.

'Why don't I bring you to your office so you can drop your bag and then I'll introduce you to the team. Unfortunately your computer is not up and running yet. It may take an hour or two, so I thought we could go for a coffee and I could begin to get you up to speed.'

'Sounds good, thanks', replied Colin, noticing that Jason spoke with a soft yet distinctive Australian accent. He had jumped to the conclusion before he introduced himself that Jason was Singaporean. Jason would later explain that he had been born to Chinese parents in Melbourne and his Singaporean wife had dragged him, kicking and screaming, back to Singapore just a year ago.

Jason led Colin past the meeting room where he had been interviewed and through the door through which he had seen Helena come just three weeks before. The intention had been for him to start earlier, but the sign-off process had taken a considerable length of time. Bank IB believed in promoting from within as much as possible, so taking on a new hire at director level was a more difficult process. In the end Colin had been through ten interviews. There had been some phone interviews with New York and Brussels and a video conference with the global head of operations, Christine Kale, in London. That one had been the most difficult to schedule but Colin was told she insisted on personally interviewing any director brought in from outside the bank. Though the interview was at ten at night, Colin almost enjoyed it. It was more a pleasant conversation than an interview. It felt to Colin as though the decision had already been made.

'So this is your office', Jason said at the door, directing Colin inside. 'As I mentioned, your computer is not ready yet', he said, gesturing to the laptop in the docking station. 'You have a login and password – I've printed these here for you – but your email doesn't work. They've promised me it will be done before lunchtime.'

'That's fine, thanks; I'm sure they'll get it up and running soon', replied Colin, though it never ceased to amaze him how large organisations could become so bureaucratic that simple things could take inexplicably and unacceptably long periods of time.

Jason took Colin to meet the other two full-time team members, who were sitting just outside his office in a bank of four cubicles, with one spare desk for visitors. Daisy Goh introduced herself, explaining that to date she had handled a lot of the project management organisation or PMO-type work.

'Once you get settled I can take you through some of the documentation and help you navigate the intranet site. Hopefully you should have access, as we requested this last week. It usually doesn't take too long to set up', she explained and went on to describe her role. In general she was responsible for putting together the presentation slides – or decks, as they were called – for steering group meetings, maintaining documentation, taking minutes, and issuing status communications, among other things. Colin was not used to the luxury of having a dedicated PMO and wondered if he could leverage Daisy's skills and experience in other ways. He had been used to taking his own minutes and issuing his own communications in other roles. He decided not to jump to any conclusions at this stage as the project size and breadth could warrant someone full time. Daisy left him with a good impression. Although she too appeared Asian, she spoke with an American accent. Colin asked what part of the USA she came from.

'I'm the only true Singaporean here', she replied, laughing. 'These guys are just blow-ins', she said, smiling and looking at her colleagues. 'I was born here and went to primary school in Singapore, but my parents thought it would be better if I was educated in the USA, so I went and lived with my aunt', she explained, as if this was quite a common thing to do. 'I went to high school and then university before coming back to Singapore to work.'

Colin found it difficult to imagine sending a child halfway around the world to be educated, especially when Singapore had a reputation for good education. He thought better of voicing his thoughts and turned his attention to Suria instead, whose gaze he had been aware of for some time. Suria Sharma sat opposite Daisy. He was the main business analyst on the project.

'You have to understand', he began quickly when Colin turned to him, 'that I could do much more on the project also. The analysis I have been doing is complex and comprehensive, and while it has real value add, I have the capacity to take on more and maybe run a stream of the project if you think it appropriate. I have a PhD in mathematics and aerospace engineering and am very capable of learning new things. I am currently studying for the PMP exam as well. I would be happy to take you through the ideas I have for how we can turn things around in the short term.'

While Colin was taken aback by Suria's unembarrassed ambition, he was happier to have someone who was obviously gunning for future promotion than someone who had little interest in progressing further. It was also the first time he had met a real rocket scientist. He was sure Suria got that a lot, so he left that ball hanging without striking it. If Suria wanted to take on more, Colin would have no problem loading him up. He would need to be careful about ensuring the quality of his deliveries, however, as he got the impression that Suria wanted to take on things in areas where he was untested. If he felt he needed to prove something he might be inclined to take on too much to continue to be effective. While Colin was happy to give someone a chance, it could not be to the detriment of the project – that would help nobody. Suria would have to start off slowly. It was immediately obvious that he would work hard, but he would also need mentoring on his communication skills if he wanted to move on in his career. He would need to learn about how to time communications appropriately, whether discussions are better held one to one or in open forum, and what message ultimately was most important to convey. The initial conversation left Colin with an understanding of Suria's ambition, a concern about his motivation and little idea of his competence.

'Let's head downstairs for a coffee', said Jason, motioning Colin back in the direction they had come from. Colin walked more slowly this time, taking in the office surroundings. The desks were in rows with low partitions between them. The floor would have seemed vast had it not been split up by the island of directors' offices in the centre, which partitioned one side from the other. In Bank IB hierarchy was more obvious than at ACB. All directors had offices and corporate titles were allocated from the bottom up. The most junior title of analyst was prefixed by either senior or junior; assistant vice-president came next, followed by vice-president, director and managing director. Total mid-range compensation could double from one title to the next, but often so too did responsibility, expectations and risk. Though the shades of grey did nothing to add character, the office space had large windows and was bright. Even though he knew he had been preoccupied when Jason had led him through a short time before, Colin was surprised that he had not noticed the tigers. In bright red and gold and with huge eyes, they were everywhere: on desks, on the walls and hanging from the ceiling. Chinese New Year was around the corner and the office was decorated to meet the Year of the Tiger.

'As soon as the last lot come down the next lot go up', said Jason, smiling. 'It seems like the Christmas decorations were only taken down last week; it was Diwali before that, and Hari Raya won't be long coming around.'

'I think it's great to see the colour, and have a bit of festivity in the office', replied Colin, though he felt like explaining to Jason that he was not fresh off the boat and had lived through many years of this. It wasn't new to him, but it did seem that the employees made a bit more of an effort than they did at ACB.

'Don't get me wrong, I like it too. In Singapore it's great that everyone celebrates all the holidays; the Hindus give each other Christmas presents and the Christians dress up in saris for Diwali. It's great.'

They took the lift down, though the café was on the ground floor, just one floor below, ordered coffee and sat in big velvet seats by the window.

'The door at the end of the stairs is a fire escape and sets off an alarm if it's opened', Jason explained. 'Your predecessor set it off once, but we'll get to that.'

Colin looked at Jason and could see that he was itching to tell him about it now rather than later. 'Why don't we start with that? I'd like to hear about my predecessor, what he's doing now and ideally get to talk to him, if that would be possible. I'm sure he could give me some candid insight into the project.'

'Well, I suppose it's as good a place to start as anywhere.' Jason sipped his cappuccino and then took a deep breath. 'The fact is that his setting off the alarm is tied up with how he left the project.'

'You're not telling me he was fired for accidentally setting off the fire alarm?'

'No, not exactly. Daniel let the project get to him. The stakeholders are pretty demanding, the project is not running smoothly and because we have a lot of dealings with London, Brussels and New York the hours are a killer. One day he was leading a steering committee meeting and was being challenged by Mike – that's Mike Gretchen, the project sponsor – when he lost it. He started screaming at Mike and then turned to each of the people in the room with him and went for them in turn one by one. Helena Biel tried to calm him down over the speakerphone from Brussels and then he began to let loose on her. He ripped the phone from the table, threw it at the wall, stormed out of the room and ran down the stairs, as if we were chasing him, setting off the alarm as he left the building.'

Colin's jaw almost hit the floor. 'Are you serious?'

'I think I lack the imagination to even make this stuff up.'

'And where is he now?'

'We think he's on some kind of paid leave and HR are dealing with it. I think they're treading carefully with this one as it could be argued that the bank was responsible for ensuring he was capable of handling the pressure. If he had been managed anything less than strictly by the book there could be recriminations. You know, they could ask were there sufficient bilateral meetings with his manager? Did he have regional local management as well as global functional management? Did he have a mentor? Was he given the right support? Were there any signs or unusual behaviour that were trivialised or ignored? The list could go on. Either way we haven't seen him since, so you will unfortunately not get to talk to him.'

'That's crazy, I've never heard anything like that before. How come no one told me before now?'

'Did you ask?' replied Jason, smiling.

Colin was beginning to see the flawed logic in his interview strategy. He looked around and took in the line beginning to form for lunchtime sandwiches; the tables were mostly full already with people dressed in business attire. The people in the café were also mostly Caucasian. Singaporeans were closer to the French in their lunchtime habits than to the Anglo-Saxons. Many would try to leave the office for lunch, whether at a hawker centre or food court selling reasonably priced local food or at a restaurant in one of the shopping malls. Having a sandwich at the café or at one's desk was generally not the done thing. Colin's eyes fell on the emergency exit door, bringing him back to his train of thought. 'How long ago did this happen? And who's been interim lead since then?'

'That was back in September, September the eleventh to be exact. I remember the date because we'd put a lot of preparation into the steering committee materials.' Colin was struck dumb for a moment. He wasn't a big believer in serendipity, fate or the coming together of the universe or anything like that, but it was very weird that Daniel was going crazy on the day he was in a windowless room being fired.

'Though Helena has been in the weeds a lot', Jason continued, 'this is only about a tenth of her overall accountability. There has been only so much she could do. I've been trying to run this delivery stream and help her with overall project management, but that's not been easy.'

'Well, that's at least something', said Colin, looking visibly relieved. 'At least I'm talking to the right person now; you must know the project inside out if you've basically been the on-the-ground lead since September.'

'That's true; that's the positive side of working on this project since September. I can sit with you, give you the lie of the land, get you up to speed and get you started.'

'And the negative?' asked Colin, sensing that there was a 'but' coming.

'I hate to lay this on you as well on your first day, when you haven't even finished your coffee, but I've also resigned.'

'Please tell me you really are joking now.'

'No, unfortunately not. Since September I've worked five nights a week past midnight. I've been on calls with New York until two in the morning. I've handled it, but it has taken its toll. On January the first, probably feeling like the start of the year was the right time for a new beginning, my wife gave me an ultimatum. She told me to leave the bank or she would leave me. I couldn't blame her really. I barely saw her at home in four months.'

'But couldn't you just take on a different role? Now, with me coming on, that should ease the burden.'

'Look, I'm sorry, but the damage is done. I've let Helena know as well, I've served three of my four weeks' notice, so I'll be here until the end of the week. Then I start a regional role at ACB where I'll work a pretty standard day.'

'You resigned three weeks ago?'

'That's right. Well, more or less; it was on a Friday.'

'Friday the eighth of January?'

'Yes, but why is that important?'

'Did you resign in the morning or the evening?'

'It was first thing in the morning, before the workshops started, so I could get some of Helena's time. Why do you ask?'

'It doesn't matter', Colin replied casually. He didn't know whether he was more annoyed with Jason or himself and he was getting too grumpy to feel he owed Jason an explanation. The first project manager went crazy the day he was fired and the second resigned the morning of his interview. The interviewers knew this and they still hired the role in Singapore. Besides the possibility that with one down and one soon to disappear they were desperate, Colin didn't understand why the role was Singapore based. He wondered if this is the reason why Roberto found it all so funny. 'What about Daisy and Suria?'

'Daisy doesn't do long hours. She does everything she's asked between nine and six, but that's it. She knows that this probably impacts on her bonus and career prospects, but that doesn't bother her. She has no promotion aspirations either, so all in all you can either accept the value she provides, replace her or augment the team further.'

'And Suria?'

'He'll do whatever you ask. He'd work through the night if you asked him but is expecting promotion as payback. He's on the long list for VP but I wouldn't promise anything if I were you as it's never easy. There are a few concerns regarding his readiness as well, but we can go through those later.' Jason looked at his watch. 'I've arranged to meet someone for lunch, but if you like I can take you through some of the project material when I get back to the office.'

When Jason had left Colin remained in the chair feeling shell-shocked. The project had almost broken the first project manager and almost broken the marriage of the second. As first days went, this one wasn't going too well. Conforming to stereotype and feeling like a drone, he joined the other pasty-white people in the queue for pasty-white bread. He then waited in line to get the elevator. It was the lunchtime rush hour in a building with two lifts and no usable stairs. He thought about both former PMs and their reasons for leaving. Though he would have loved to think that bad management was causing the requirement to work such long hours and that he would be able to right all wrongs, he had the feeling that it was simply the nature of the beast and the result of running a global project from Singapore. He had run a project at ACB that had involvement from the New York office and at that time he alternated between Singapore evenings and mornings for calls, but including Brussels and London meant that that solution could not work if all regions had to be represented. He'd expected to participate in calls a few nights a week, but calls until midnight five nights a week was pretty excessive.

Back in his office he logged onto his computer and found that there were already a hundred or so emails waiting for his attention. Looking at a few it was obvious that he had been added to email distribution lists a few days prior to his arrival. Scrolling through his inbox his eyes hit on the email he was hoping to see. The subject line read 'Handover material'. He clicked on the message that had been sent by Jason that same morning.

Hi Colin,

Welcome on board. Once you've settled and have time please let me know and I will take you through some of this material. It could be in better condition but, as I will explain, this is the second handover within the space of a few months and things have been pretty hectic. Each of the items in the list below contains a hyperlink that will open the named document stored on the intranet:

- Project Charter
- Project Initiation Document (PID)
- Scope, Design and High-Level Plan
- Project Governance and Communication
- Stakeholder Matrix
- RAID Log
- Detailed Project Plan

Best regards,
Jason Tan

Colin clicked on the first link, which took him to the project charter. This is the document that is used to authorise the project when it is first proposed. In a way it is the contract for delivery owned by the sponsor, making him or her accountable for the budget provided. Even before he opened the document, the first thing that hit him was the date on which it was last saved, 6 February 2009, a little under a year ago. It contained what would generally be expected in such a document: a very short summary on the background and opportunity, the objectives, a few words of business case, short scope statement, very high-level schedule, a summary approach and the key risks, assumptions, issues and dependencies, or RAID for short. He could not help but wonder whether it was still valid. It looked as though it had everything that was needed at the time. Including the programme manager, named as Daniel Klerk, all of the names were already familiar to him. The sponsor was Mike Gretchen, Helena Biel was head of change, and IT manager was Roberto Giovanni. The budget was a round $20 million and the schedule showed that the first deliveries should have already been implemented.

He clicked on the PID and scrolled quickly through it, just picking up the headings as he went. He wondered what would be in the document. Though he had encountered documents with this name before, organisations would often have customised content or use completely different names for documents with which he was familiar. In ACB the PID would have been called the project management plan. If he related it to the theory of project management, as defined by some standardisation organisations, it would have gone some way to filling the clinical definition of a project management plan, in other words a good description of the 'what, when, where and why'. It had expanded versions of what was to be done, when it would be completed, where it would be implemented, and why it was needed in the first place; in project management parlance the scope, schedule and business case. It also contained some of the 'how'; it covered how delivery would be managed, governed and executed and how changes would be monitored, as well as how the project would be controlled.

The scope, design and high-level plan looked, at least at first glance, to be a version of some areas of the PID in a presentation deck format.

The project governance and communication deck was informative as it was the most recent document. It showed a programme organisation chart that already had Colin's name filled in as overall project manager and a view of how the project delivery streams were structured. It had an outline of the roles and responsibilities of the key team members and a high-level view of how the governance was run, with a steering group overseeing the project delivery, a working group for managing the delivery of the work packages and some further meetings within the work streams or sub-projects. It also had some clear summaries of the individual work streams.

He opened the RAID log next. This had 580 risks, assumptions, issues or dependencies logged. While it was unfortunate that there were so many, it was great that it gave almost a blow-by-blow history of the trials and tribulations of the project since its conception. What was more worrying, though, was that it had been Daniel Klerk who had been so diligent; the last entry was in September 2009 and he had made this himself.

Colin could not tell whether the stakeholder matrix was up to date or not. It had been modified as recently as the previous day but still named Daniel Klerk as the project manager. As he opened it he had a flashback to his interview. He had said back then that the first thing he would do was to meet with all the stakeholders. He looked at his watch and saw it was already past six. Jason had not come by because Colin had become so immersed in the documentation that he had not gone out to ask him to come in to talk. He had only four more days with Jason on board, and he would have to figure out how best to use his time while Jason was still there. He realised also how impractical it was to meet with all stakeholders first. He could not go to see Mike Gretchen knowing no more than he had when he was interviewed. For some reason the calendar function in his email application was not working yet, so he did not even have a way of setting up a meeting with him or the other stakeholders.

When he had gone through all the other links he looked at the saved copy of the detailed project plan, saw it had been last saved six months ago, looked at his watch again and decided that he should call it a day. He felt tired. It was as if he was competing in a repeating triathlon. He had completed the swim again and was gratefully out of the water, he'd reached his bike and was mounting for a long cycle, knowing he'd have to run a marathon at the end of the ride. He realised that he had not spoken to Clara all day. He turned to the phone and reached for the receiver, but before he picked it up it rang. There was no name on the display.

'Hello, this is Colin speaking.'

'Hello Colin, welcome on board', said Helena enthusiastically. 'How has your first day been so far?'

'Well, it's been pretty informative, and I have to say somewhat surprising.'

'Yes, well, swings and roundabouts I suppose, but we're all glad you're on board', said Helena. 'I just wanted to call to help you out a little because I'm getting a strange message from your calendar when I invite you to meetings. I've asked my secretary to raise it with the help desk on your behalf and they've said it should be fixed by the morning. In the meantime, I've sent you today's meetings by email.'

'Oh, eh, thanks for that, but I had planned to …'

'Sorry, Colin, Christine Kale has just walked into my office. As I said, great to have you on board. I'll talk to you in twenty minutes at the status meeting. I've sent you the deck you can use going forward.'

Colin sat looking at the phone in shock. It had already started.

4

Project Fundamentals

It wasn't until eleven the next morning that Jason put his head around Colin's door. Colin had been in the office since eight. He had woken at six thirty as usual, even though he hadn't gone to bed until after midnight. He thought Clara was asleep when he entered the bedroom so he had changed quietly and tried to slip into bed unnoticed. As he did she had rolled over to her side of the bed, away from him and showing him her back. He had put the symbolism down to his own paranoia and the tales of madness and marital strife from the day. He then fell into a restless sleep.

'Good morning. It seems you had a bit of a baptism of fire last night', started Jason cheerily as he strolled into Colin's office.

'Morning Jason. I had hoped to go through some of the things we covered last night as well as the handover material with you this morning', he said glancing at his watch, regretting it even as he did so.

'Well, sorry if I'm later than you expected but I spent some time with my one-year-old daughter before coming in. I was on the calls with you until eleven last night and I haven't got to see her much lately.'

'Of course, I understand. That's fine. I completely understand. I'm a bit tired myself. Of course I want to squeeze as much out of you as I can before you leave.'

'No worries, Colin.'

'And you're right', Colin went on, feeling that the air he himself had frozen had already thawed a little. 'It was a baptism of fire. I couldn't believe Helena asked me to present the status update for the project when I hadn't even been in the bank a day.'

'That's Helena', replied Jason. 'She has really high expectations and will throw you into the deep end just to see if you can swim. She does it in a safe environment, though; she's standing at the side with a life ring just in case.'

'All the same, it felt pretty intense.'

'Get used to it!'

'Would you mind giving me a quick recap of the meetings in terms of what they have been set up for and what's generally expected?'

'Sure. The first meeting is the weekly status meeting for the project. Generally Helena chairs it, but you will run the agenda and present the materials. There is a standard pack that we update with IT on a weekly basis. It's worth making sure you're on the same page as IT before this meeting as I've seen it get rough when we were not already aligned.'

'I'm guessing you're going to tell me there's a scheduled pre-meeting for the IT PM and business PM to sort out any differences beforehand.'

'You guessed it. We generally have this on the Friday before. It may seem inefficient and "a meeting for a meeting", but the Friday meeting is pretty productive and we work through with IT what was or was not achieved the week before and what's on the agenda for the following week.'

'Does Roberto Giovanni attend this as well?'

'No. Serge Baranov attends, but Roberto attends the status update with Helena. There is usually some subject matter expertise – SME – representation as well but generally we call this "the Helena meeting" because its purpose is to update her on progress and escalate things to her that she can help with. It's also for Helena to give direction. We generally go through what was accomplished in the last week and what we want to get done the next week. We go through the milestones of the plan and the top issues and risks.'

'Okay, so pretty standard stuff then. I'm guessing the next is a weekly meeting for Helena's direct reports?'

'Yes, this is the change management team meeting. There's generally no material to prepare for this iteration of the meeting. If there are issues that span across the portfolio they can be raised there so that the other project managers can get a heads up, for example if IT are scheduling maintenance at a particular time or if there are any cross-programme dependencies. Helena generally cascades any information that she has from Christine Kale, the head of ops, at this meeting as well.'

'What do you mean by "this iteration" of the meeting?'

'The management team meets once a week but cycles through four topics in a month. Yesterday's meeting was for portfolio governance, next week the focus is on cost and budget, the week after on people and the week after that it's a general management meeting with topics raised in advance by team members for discussion. It cycles through these topics.'

'And the meeting directly after that, run by Serge, is a meeting for systems integration testing. Is this once a week as well?'

'Sorry to tell you, Colin, but this is daily at the moment', Jason replied and although he sounded apologetic, Colin could not help but feel that he was happy at the thought that he would soon be leaving it behind. 'We're in crisis mode at the moment in SIT: things aren't going too well, as I am sure you picked up.'

'Yes this was all too clear. To be honest, after that call I thought that the status update we gave earlier in the evening was over-sanitised.'

'That was as strongly worded as could be managed with Serge's agreement', Jason said with a sigh as if it was a regular occurrence that status would be watered down to save confrontation. Colin couldn't help but feel that it was going to be a pretty rocky road ahead.

'I've managed to get half an hour in Mike Gretchen's diary in ten minutes. Do you have time, say at one o'clock, to go through some of the handover material?'

'That's fine. I had a meeting scheduled with the test lead but I'll postpone that until later.'

'Any advice before I meet Mike? Of all the people who interviewed me he seemed the most aggressive.'

'Mike generally decides on a part to play and he takes on the role with gusto. He's like one of these method actors who immerse themselves in a role. He was probably playing the "tough interviewer". I've seen him play "empathetic team leader", "supportive sponsor" and plenty of other roles. It depends on what he has decided. It's great if you can influence him, as having him on your side is a great asset. He can be "vendor driver" or "barrier destroyer" – it's fun to watch, but I just wonder if he knows it's so noticeable. Of course the downside is you never know whether you'll meet Dr Jekyll or Mr Hyde. What is consistent, though, is that he cares about results and he values knowledge. Whatever you do, don't try to bluff him. If you do and he spots it he'll lose all respect for you. Just play it straight – he may not always himself, but it's what he expects.'

It was not a long walk to Mike's office, which was slightly bigger than the directors' offices, matching his MD status. It was in the corner, with two windows on the inside walls, and the outside walls were made of glass. Colin couldn't help but think of the psychology and incentives course he once attended. The extra few centimetres of space and the view of the runway were a positive contribution towards Mike's job satisfaction, whether he knew it or not. Seen from the outside it was pretty silly, but from the inside just some of the things dreams are made of. Sad, really. Mike was on the phone.

'Sorry, he's behind schedule. I'm Jennifer Ng, Mike's assistant. And you must be Colin.'

'Hi, Jennifer. Yes, that's right, we spoke on the phone last night. Sorry I couldn't send the invite directly but my calendar wasn't working yesterday. It seems to be working now though.'

'Well, if that's the only on-boarding teething problem you've had you've done pretty well. When I joined it took a week before I even had a phone!' Jennifer said, smiling at Colin with unnaturally blue eyes. He found himself staring and finally came to the conclusion that the colour was from coloured contact lenses. Just as he was beginning to feel awkward the door opened and Mike walked out with his hand outstretched in greeting.

'Colin, we've finally managed to get you on board. Welcome. Welcome to Bank Investissement Belgique and to the project.' Mike bellowed so loudly that half the office heard his enthusiastic welcome as he squeezed Colin's hand like an old friend. 'Come in, come in', he said enthusiastically. 'Take a seat.'

Mike pulled out a chair for Colin at the round table beside his desk. There was a small shelf beside it with little crystal plaques for various business achievements and a bowling trophy from a recent team event. Mike paused as a plane took off before continuing.

'So how are you settling in?'

'Well, I think Jason put it well when he said this morning that I was getting a baptism of fire. It's pretty obvious that there's a lot going on.'

'And how do you think it's going?'

'I can see some issues, certainly, but to be honest I would prefer if you could share your views. I'm still forming my own and I'd like to first do some more digging before I can fully form them and articulate them with some degree of confidence.'

'That's fair enough. As you might have gathered by now, there are some delays. The testing IT is doing is taking too long as far as I'm concerned. From my perspective there's too much bureaucracy and people are hiding behind so-called methodology. We asked for a system to be built that does some calculations and has a process flow built in. How hard can that be? Now they have about ten types of testing. It seems over-engineered. Can you explain to me why they need to test ten times?'

Colin was unsure if Mike was asking him a rhetorical question or whether he actually wanted an answer. Mike looked pretty agitated, as if he had had it up to his ears with project management speak.

'I look at software development like building a house. To start with the bricks had better be properly made because no matter how well you stack them the house will fall down if they're not made right. It would also be pretty expensive to find this out once the house is complete, so some one better have checked their quality. This is the unit testing where the developers test each other's coded modules.' Colin still couldn't read Mike's face. Either Colin was teaching his grandmother to suck eggs or Mike was generally interested in the analogy, but either way he waited for Colin to go on.

'Once the bricks are deemed good quality they are stacked to make the house using cement. The systems integration testing or SIT checks that the cement works with the bricks, the roof is compatible with the walls and the walls hold it up. It checks that the taps connect to the water source and water flows when you turn them on. The user acceptance testing – UAT – has the users come in and take a look. They turn on the water and though water flows they may complain that it is cold instead of hot. That the front door opens outwards instead of inwards, and the windows are single glazed. If the user asked for all of these things in the beginning and they were priced into the building contract, then these are problems that the builder needs to fix, and if not they are design gaps and change requests that the user will have to pay for if they want things changed.'

'That's fine, and I buy all of that', Mike answered, 'but irrespective of whether I asked for it in the first place, if I find something I can't live without, the developers should just go away and fix it as fast as possible without the need for a lengthy discussion to determine if it is a change request or not.'

Colin remembered back to the SIT call of the night before. Much of the time was spent referring back to the functional specification and triaging the problems found into change requests or software bugs. He didn't intervene, as he wanted to listen and learn before trying to make any changes. He did, however, feel that the triage process should first focus on whether an issue is critical or high, and only second on whether or not it is a change request. For example, it was contentious whether one of the problems, which had been debated for twenty minutes during the call the night before, was a bug or a change request. In the end it was agreed that it was a change request and low priority so should be deferred. While that might be frustrating on a call during the working day, at close to midnight it was simply unacceptable.

'I think you have a point. The change request versus defect debate is necessary. If they were not asked to build something they're going to charge us to get it done. This, however, is secondary to the priority debate. If the problem is low priority we should not be spending any time on it. We first need to triage based on priority and then, if necessary, decide if the problem is a change request or a bug. I'll take an action to have the process changed from tonight's call, assuming I can get our IT colleagues to agree.'

'If you can't, let me know, please.'

Colin had initially been surprised that Mike got straight down to business. No sooner had he sat down than he was straight into pushing through changes in the way things were done. As he thought about it, however, it was exactly the way the interview had gone and in line with Jason's view on how Mike operated. His role in this instance was 'project sponsor' and he was in character from the handshake. Colin wondered how Mike would define his role.

'The sponsors of the projects I've run in the past have seen their roles pretty differently. How would you define your role as sponsor?'

'Bottom line is that I am accountable for the change in the business that this project is to bring about. I am accountable for every dollar spent and I own the success or failure of the project.'

'Well we're in it together then from that perspective', Colin ventured, 'we succeed or fail together.'

'Not exactly', Mike said with a wry smile. 'We're tied up in this together right now sure enough and I want to support you to ensure that you are successful, as I will be successful too, but if I see that you're not delivering you'll be failing on your own. You like analogies, so try this one. If the project is a war and you begin to fail, you may lose the battle. That's your war over. I'll just have to find another soldier to send to the front. If I keep doing that, however, someone will shoot me. On that basis you should have no doubt that I am behind you and I do want to see you succeed.'

'You are, as you mentioned, accountable for the budget. How does this look?'

'The original budget was twenty million dollars over three years. The approval process took some time in the first year and we were under by about a million at the end of the year.

It looks that this year we're on track to spend the five million, so we are on target as far as I can see.'

Colin wasn't so sure but thought better of discussing this further until he had the numbers to back up his gut feeling.

'You mentioned your frustration with testing. Is there anything else on your mind that you think I should be looking at?'

'As sponsor I said I was accountable for the business outcome, or, said another way, I am responsible for the business benefits being delivered. Right now everyone is focused on the project delivery. Every steering committee I attend I wonder with all the focus on project delivery if we have forgotten about what we set out to deliver in the first place. It seems the users are the ones driving the changes, but this project should be removing the need for some of their roles. Are they the right people to be driving the requirements?'

Colin suppressed a smile. Mike was referring back to the interview, in which he had advocated the need for a target operating model or TOM and for this to be driven by people with less skin in the game. He was, of course, putting it forward as his own idea. Colin was fine with that; Mike would support it more strongly if he felt it was his own.

'How do you think it should be driven?'

'I think we need to have our future state operating model documented and agreed. This should be done by someone independent of the users but with strong collateral experience in multiple environments, specifically in our own.'

'Have you considered getting a specialist company to come in? Quite often they will have an off-the-shelf best practice TOM that they would tailor to our environment, taking account of potential regulatory changes and segregation of duties.'

'Have a look at what we have so far and come back to me with a proposal. Colin, it's been good seeing you again. I'm glad you're on board and I know we can win this war together.'

And with this pep talk Mike got up, signalling that the meeting was over, and opened the door. It looked as though the whirlwind that had tried to blow him to pieces during his interview had turned into a tail wind – for now at least. He wondered about the code being tested. He had assumed that testing was based on functions documented in a functional specification, written based on detailed business require-ments, which would have been created from a TOM. This was pretty standard stuff. If he had heard Mike correctly it could be that the TOM either did not exist or was inadequate. If this was the case the very plan to which the house was being built might not exist or might be seriously flawed. If this were the case there would likely be a significant premium to be paid.

He needed to meet with Serge as soon as possible to agree the testing triage approach. This was something that could have the biggest short-term impact on progress. If he already had a relationship with Serge it could have been as quick as sending an email, but starting with an email to suggest new and better ways of doing things was probably the wrong way to build a relationship with the IT team. When he got back to his desk he opened his calendar to schedule a meeting with Serge. Entering Serge's name brought up his availability. The calendar showed a maroon colour right up to nine in the evening Singapore time, which meant that Serge would be out of the office until then. He obviously only started work at nine in the morning in New York. This was going to be difficult. The first hour was blue. Serge either had a meeting scheduled or was blocking the time to get some work done undisturbed. Colin requested the meeting in the first available slot between ten and ten thirty in the evening, which meant that there would be an hour between the end of this call and the testing meeting. While he thought about how he would be spending his evening – and would likely be spending his evenings for the foreseeable future – Suria knocked at the door.

'I was just wondering if you would like to go for lunch?'

Colin did not feel like another limp sandwich and had no idea what other options were available. He also suddenly realised that he was pretty hungry.

'Sounds like a great idea. I'm just about ready now if you are.'

'Yes, I'm ready. We can go to the café downstairs if you like; they make very good sandwiches.'

As Suria was assuming that Colin would conform to stereotype, Colin thought he'd return the ball. 'I was thinking of Indian food if there are any good places around.'

There was a queue outside the Indian restaurant. The choice of restaurants was limited and it turned out that the Indian restaurant was one of the best options.

'Once the new shopping mall opens in the next building there should be a better selection, but now there are not many places to go', Suria explained as they waited in line.

They both filled their plates at the buffet before sitting down. It was just what Colin had been hoping for. There was some great buttered dal, a range of naan and roti breads, basmati rice, as well as various meat and vegetable options in creamy curry sauces or simply lightly spiced. The range of food available in Singapore was one of its greatest strengths, in his view. The breadth of Asian flavours that could be found was extraordinary. Judging by the customers at the other tables it was clear that the food was seen as pretty authentic. Lost in the atmosphere and flavours, Colin and Suria spent the better part of lunch enjoying the food and talking food, culture and travel before Colin even brought up the project.

'Have you been on the project from the beginning?' asked Colin finally.

'I have not only been on the project since the beginning but I have been on it through two name changes already. The name I liked best was CASAR or Collateral Assessment, Segregation and Remediation.'

'Why was the name changed?'

'It was partly because the programme was technically stopped before it was restarted, but it had mostly to do with the "Segregation" piece in the name. The idea of the last sponsor, who has since left the bank, was more to build up expertise and process centralisation rather than moving processes away from a collateral central area and functionalise them across the bank. It was a total change of approach.'

'Sounds like moving from empire building to empire destruction.'

'You could say that but, either way, when Mike took on sponsorship he took up the new direction.'

'Were you doing business analysis from the beginning?'

'Yes, the business analyst role was pretty important from the beginning and that was my focus. I ran the "as-is" analysis to document the way things are currently being done today. I was responsible for putting the target operating model or TOM together, which ominously resulted in the project being stopped temporarily. You should recognise, however, that it was done in the context of the old sponsor direction, so was very well received in his area. I suppose that could be expected, however, as it increased the responsibility of people within that group.'

'Did you then take the TOM and build business requirements from these?'

'Yes, exactly. I wrote the business requirements documents or BRDs based on the TOM, interviewing the stakeholders and leveraging the "as-is" documentation so that I could build requirements for automating these processes. Once I finished the BRDs I moved on to the functional requirements documents, the FRDs', explained Suria.

'I presume the FRDs are pretty standard in that they take the BRD requirements and describe them as more detailed modules that the IT team can write technical specifications against for coding?' Colin knew he was asking the obvious, but it seemed already that he could not take anything for granted.

'Yes, exactly, that's originally how they were created', replied Suria but looking a little unsure, as if he was holding back something.

'You say "originally"; were they changed in some way since then?'

'Well the original functional specifications were written against the original BRDs, which in turn were written against the original TOM, but as the original TOM was moving towards centralisation we had to change the functional specifications to rectify this. Whereas before everything that could be loosely aligned to a collateral process was to be centralised, the change in direction was to remove everything but the core collateral processes. As an example, collateral settlement was previously to be centralised with the collateral team, but in the new model it was to be moved to the settlements team. Quite a lot of processes, actually, are to be functionally aligned in this way in the new model.'

'So I presume that the TOM, FRDs and BRDs were all rewritten?'

'No, it was decided to leave the TOM alone as so much time had been spent on it already and the BRDs and FRDs were marked up instead. You know, a red pen taken through some of the old functionality relating to centralisation and some extra functionalisation elements appended. So basically some pieces were added and some pieces struck out by the users since there was a new approach.'

'So who created the new TOM and requirements based on the new model of moving generic functions such as settlement and booking out of the collateral processing group?' asked Colin, as if he had not heard what Suria had just said. He did not want to believe that there was such a flaw in the project design.

'This was not done in the end as it took about a year all in all to create the first TOM and requirements. There was a view that if we did it all again we would get nowhere, so we were asked to move directly to the technical specifications and coding based on marked-up functional specifications.'

Colin began to feel a little unwell and he knew it had nothing to do with his delicious Indian meal. 'So what you're saying is that the coding for this release was requested based on functional specifications, marked up by committee, that do not tie back to signed-off business requirements and that are not related to a TOM that anyone has agreed.'

'Said like that it's pretty harsh, but yes, that's an accurate statement.'

'Okay', replied Colin, slowly and thoughtfully elongating each vowel. 'That might explain the lengthy "change request versus defect" conversations then. If the users are expecting delivery of standard functionality and it is not documented as a deliverable, then confusion is going to reign.'

'Yes, there have been a lot of moving parts. It doesn't help either that the people in the business who were responsible for the first iterations of these documents have mostly moved on as well, so the users who are testing expect something different too', said Suria, obviously feeling he was about to go the way of the proverbial messenger.

'So in most projects I have worked on, the test cases or test scripts are run to try out the future processes and system functionality and these are tested by the users in user acceptance testing or UAT. They're normally written against the original user requirements in the business requirements document. If the BRDs are not available in any useful form, how were the test cases written?'

'The users wrote them based on their current processes.'

'But if they're testing the system against the current processes, the best that can be hoped for is to have a semi-automated version of what exists today', sighed Colin, who was by now pretty exasperated. 'I think we'd better head back to the office. I have a meeting with Jason this afternoon too.'

'Yes, but before we go I just want to ensure you understand that this is not all document related. It is, of course, a problem, but remember that we are only in the systems integration testing phase and we are running into these problems. The vendor has essentially not been able to deliver against FRDs that they were part of writing and marking up. The functional knowledge is so low in the vendor team that every line of code is a negotiation.'

Colin had heard enough and they got up to leave. Though the office was less than five minutes' walk from the restaurant, Colin's shirt was stuck to his back by the time he reached the air-conditioned building. The humidity, along with the heat, made the walk feel more like a swim. He was a few minutes late for his meeting with Jason and this time Jason was waiting for him.

'Did you go for a run?' Jason asked with a smile.

'Good one', replied Colin, faking a belly laugh. 'I'll never get used to the heat here.'

'You do look pretty hot', Daisy interjected, popping her head up from her desk.

'Thanks a lot', replied Colin a little sarcastically, thinking that a bit too much notice was being taken of his dishevelled appearance.

Daisy smiled. 'I didn't mean it that way!'

It took a moment for the penny to drop. Colin wasn't used to hearing double entendres in the office. That might have gone down well in some Anglo-Saxon working environments in the past, but it was usually not welcome in Singapore.

'I didn't mean it that way, either', he said.

'The thing is, you have got to slow down', continued Daisy. 'You have to learn to take your time or it will be over before you know it. You have to learn to adapt instead of trying to just move your way of life with you. Look around next time you're walking back from lunch and gauge the pace people are walking. My bet is you are walking twice as fast as anyone else. Better still, count how many people you overtake.'

Colin had to laugh. He'd been in Singapore a long time but had never changed his habit of walking quickly. Walking was a way to get from point A to point B and slowing down felt strange.

'You might get where you are going more quickly', Daisy continued, 'but when you do get there you're wet and red-faced and need time to cool down.'

'I see your point but, honestly, in that heat at midday, whether I'm strolling, sauntering or doing the quick-step I'm still going to arrive red-faced and sweating like a pig. I've learned to accept it and so might you', Colin retorted good-humouredly. He enjoyed the banter and was a little surprised by Daisy's forthrightness. It was probably a habit she picked up in the USA, he thought; Singaporeans were often more reserved. Once he sat down in the office Colin printed copies of the documents that he wanted to go through with Jason.

'I've printed a few copies of the documents you sent me through', began Colin as he slid a small bundle of double-sided printed documents to Jason. 'I thought it would be a good idea if we could go through these together so I can get the chance to ask you a few questions while you're still here.'

'No problem', replied Jason, 'though I think they should be pretty self-explanatory.'

'I think it's more context that I need, and a bit more under-standing of what's up to date and what needs to be made current. Take this project charter, for example. It looks like it was last updated last year, but even that seems a bit odd as it shows Mike Gretchen as the sponsor but the original project objectives are still captured here.'

'We updated it with Mike as the sponsor once he came on board.'

'But didn't the project objectives also change when he started? The charter describes process centralisation, but we're trying to functionalise or distribute the processes to groups already in place.'

'That's true, I suppose', replied Jason, sounding somewhat nonchalant, 'but there was no point in updating it fully as the funding had been signed off and provided.'

Colin decided not to go any farther with the questioning, as it really was not going to help. It wasn't his job to educate Jason now but rather to get as good a handover as he could from him. He had just a few days left with him and he needed to keep him on side. It would be very easy for him to take some sick days instead of coming to work in the next couple of days. The charter should have been updated with the new objectives: he knew it and so did Jason. The agreed charter should be the basis of all project deliverables. Success would be judged against the objectives and business case proposed in the charter. In his view it was the charter that documented his own objectives as project manager.

'Are the project initiation document and the others also based on the original design?'

'Keeping the documentation up to date has not really been the focus as we've had burning fires to deal with. As you know, the SIT is not going well, so it's been all hands on deck to get things working.'

While Colin had picked up on this, he had also realised that the SIT problems were a symptom of the problem rather than the problem itself. The code that had been written had been written based on possibly contradicting objectives and a design that was at best unstructured, most likely inadequate and of poor quality, and at worst requiring a rewrite by a different vendor. He knew already that he would have to make some unpopular recommendations if he was to get the project back on track and he was unsure how palatable this would be to the wider stakeholder group.

'The project initiation document has quite a lot in it', continued Colin, trying to sound more positive. 'Did you write this?'

'It has the authors and contributors listed on the third page', Jason replied as he swung his copy around, showing Colin the list. 'It was a joint effort between Suria and me.'

'Great, thanks, I see that now', said Colin, beginning to feel that this was going to be a painful process as long as Jason continued to be defensive. 'Could you take me through it, perhaps, rather than me questioning it?'

'Sure. At Bank IB before budgets are approved we need to submit the charter we just discussed but also have it backed up by the PID. The charter acts as the contract between the sponsor and the bank senior executives who agree the budget. The PID forms the contract between the project manager and the sponsor. The charter sets out what's going to be done, when it will be delivered, who will be account-able and responsible for delivery, and what the benefits are going to be. The PID in Bank IB is an expansion of this and gives the "how" on each of the areas in the charter. Where the charter outlines what's going to be delivered, the PID outlines how it's going to be delivered. Stop me, please, if you know all this already.'

'No, please go on. While a lot of it is standard, different banks expect things to be done in different ways. What I'm hearing so far is that your PID is similar to what many stand-ards refer to as the "project management plan", would that be right?'

'That's more or less it', conceded Jason, 'but it doesn't cover everything one for one.'

'Please go on and explain it as though it's new to me; that will help me learn about Bank IB even through the things I know already on the project management side.'

'Okay, as I said the PID here is the "how" to each area covered by the charter. So where the charter says what is going to be delivered, the PID covers how it will be managed. It details how schedule, communication, risks, resources, quality and cost are all managed. The good thing about this is that much of this is standardised within Bank IB so you can more or less copy and paste from other projects' PIDs and follow them as an instruction manual almost.'

'As I said, that's pretty helpful to me. I'm guessing there are standard templates that you use as well for a lot of your documentation so you don't have to reinvent the wheel every time', asked Colin, encouraging Jason to go on now that he felt he was gaining some momentum.

'Yeah, there is a lot of that. We have standard cost, resource and risk management documentation. We also have standard templates to show governance, roles and responsibilities, and all of that stuff.'

The conversation was helping Colin to understand what he would need to do to get some understanding of the project. Much of the PID could act as a guide for the way things were done in Bank IB and the parts that related to expansion of the high-level scope, plan and benefits would need to be updated.

'Okay, thanks. I think I'm pretty comfortable with the PID. Could we move on to the two presentation decks entitled "Scope, Design and High-Level Plan" and "Project Governance and Communication"? Correct me if I'm wrong, but it looks like these contain pretty similar information as the PID but in a slide deck format instead.'

'That's true. This is a standard deck that all projects have. Usually it's used as the first steering group deck. The steering committee or STC is chaired by Mike and is attended by all senior stakeholders. Each member is usually taken through this one by one before the STC and their feedback is woven into the deck. Sounds like a painful process, I'm sure, but it is pretty important here, at least for the kick-off, that everybody is in agreement on what we want to do and how we plan to do it.'

'Did this presentation go through the same process?'

'Yes and no', admitted Jason. 'The first iteration of it did and most of that first iteration is still in these papers. As with the charter and PID, the scope reflects the initial intentions and not the current goal. This updated version has only been updated for new governance and stakeholders. I did this just before you arrived so you could see in the governance charts where you fit in and who holds the main roles and responsibilities currently.'

'Well, thanks for that, it is helpful to see this in the organisation chart. I can see here it shows Daisy as running the project management office, you as lead on the OTC stream, and a "TBD" against the three other streams. Are these TBDs open roles today and are we hiring for them?'

'No. The intention was that once OTC trades were delivered as part of this release I would move on to the next stream. The intention was always for your role to be hands-on, delivering each of these with assistance from one stream lead for the area that was in focus at the time.'

'And what about your role? Has this been opened by HR?'

'I think this may be one of your first interactions with HR on the hiring side here', answered Jason with a smile.

'Ah, I see. What about Suria? I can't find him anywhere on the organisation chart.'

'These ones usually go down as far as the stream leads only. Business analysts, subject matter experts and operations or "business as usual" change assistance is covered in the stakeholder list.'

Both Colin and Jason flicked to this next document. It was printed from a spreadsheet with people's names in the column on the furthest left followed by department, location, project role, functional role and comments.

'This is one document that is up to date with everyone who has been on the project', said Jason, almost proudly.

Colin did not want to burst his bubble, but he could not make out from the list who was on the project now and who had already left. Jason had kindly added Colin's name in the project manager role, but the last project manager was also there, as was Mike Gretchen and his predecessor. He decided to go through this line by line with Suria.

'Is there anything that indicates these stakeholders' level of interest or influence in the project or something that describes their level of support?' asked Colin hopefully; such information would really help him navigate the conversations he would need to have in the coming days and weeks.

'Yes, actually there is', beamed Jason. 'It is hidden from the printout as it is a bit sensitive. You need to unhide some columns. It's password protected, so I'll send this to you after our meeting.'

'Great, that would be very helpful, thank you', said Colin, visibly pleased at the surprise. 'The last document I think we should have a look at today is the RAID log.'

'To be honest, Colin I think you would be better going through the RAID log on your own and coming to me with questions. It covers a lot up to when Daniel left but has not been updated since. I sent it to you for a few reasons: first it is really detailed and puts the project history in context, and second it is one of the standard format documents that you might want to use going forward.'

'Okay, so are there any other issues documented anywhere?'

'We started SIT testing about then, so any issues that are raised are documented as either defects or change requests. We have been focusing on these rather than the softer-type issues and risks.'

Colin felt like asking Jason if he meant the softer issues like the project team falling to pieces, an absence of baselined foundation documentation and no clear direction, but he bit his tongue.

5

Work–Life Balance

Colin left work on the dot of six o'clock. He had decided that morning as he left for the office that he would need to build some kind of a routine if this was going to work for any length of time. It would not be a routine that would inspire envy, but it would at least be one he thought he could live with for a while.

'You've finished early', said Clara with a smile as he walked into the kitchen where she was preparing dinner.

'I'm certainly home earlier than last night, but unfortunately I'm not finished. My calls start again at eight tonight and go on again until after midnight.'

'Well, at least you're home', replied Clara.

He had been right the night before when he guessed he was imagining Clara's annoyance at his late return home. She had not even heard him. At breakfast that morning they had talked through the challenges that the job would bring and they had agreed to take it in steps. She was supportive and knew that in the job environment of the 'Great Recession' (as it was beginning to be called) Colin was lucky to have a solid job.

'Yeah, that's true, but even though this is only the second night I'm already wondering how sustainable this is going to be. Have the kids already eaten?'

'Yes, they're just putting their pyjamas on. At least I hope they are – it's gone too quiet up there for my liking.'

'Okay, I'll get them to bed and we can at talk some more over dinner.'

As the kids had already had their bath he read them a story together and put each of them to bed, following a routine that seemed to get longer every night. He understood Jason's perspective on spending time with his daughter and he was determined not to sacrifice his time with his kids for the sake of the job. He would have to strike the right balance. Clara had chosen to be a stay-at-home mum and she had left a pretty senior position at one of the top five consulting firms when their first child, Joe, was born. He was now four and their daughter, Marie, was two.

Clara's experience had always been a support to him. They would bounce ideas off each other and play devil's advocate to see where their ideas could be challenged. While Clara was away from office life, and didn't want to return, she remained good counsel. As far as the children were concerned, Colin had always been involved and he didn't want that to change. He finally got both children settled by seven fifteen, leaving him forty-five minutes for dinner with Clara before his calls started.

'That took a while', Clara said as they sat down at the patio table. It was still warm and humid, but the ceiling fan gave some comfort in the evening air. The house was far from the hum of the city and in the garden the cicadas and crickets fought for airtime.

'Marie was a bit unsettled. I had to sing her that song ten times before she even closed her eyes.'

'Would you like a glass of wine with your pasta? It's nice and cool.'

'I'd love one, but if I do I'll be struggling even more to stay active and awake for the next five hours', said Colin with a sigh. 'As I said earlier, I'm not sure how sustainable this is going to be.'

'Why did they decide to hire the position here at all? Don't get me wrong, I'm glad you have a good job, but it seems that running this project from here has some pretty obvious disadvantages and from what you mentioned this morning they've already been feeling the impact.'

'I think it's because Mike is the sponsor and likes to feel he has control. Having the project manager in the same location may not mean that the project is in control, but at least there is someone close by he can give the hairdryer treatment to.'

'Again, Colin, as you mentioned this morning, it might be better if the project manager were not in his proximity to save the bank some legal fees if he still believes that kind of behaviour is acceptable', replied Clara, who did not like the idea of her husband having to sit in front of some screaming man who she imagined as a red-faced monster with bulging veins.

'I didn't really mean that last bit seriously. Mike's been supportive so far and it's clear that he does listen. Though, point taken, it is going to be difficult. I've blocked out my calendar now every day from six to eight in the evening and shown this time as out of office. It doesn't mean that I will never have to do a call at this time but I need to draw a line in the sand somewhere. And I've blocked out Friday after six completely.'

'Let's see how long that lasts', said Clara, doubtfully, pouring herself a glass of wine.

'Yes, let's see. It seems to me not to be an unreasonable start considering I'll be available practically all my other waking hours. The timing has the advantage of being around London lunchtime and before New York gets in, so I think I'm pretty safe. I have my first call with my new boss tonight, so I'll discuss it with her as well.'

It was about five to eight when Colin closed the door of the spare room behind him. He needed to log in to his laptop, which he had lugged from the office with him, and connect to the virtual private network or VPN that gave him the same access as he had at the office. He also had a headset that allowed him to make and take calls through the office network. It reminded him of a Patrick Chappatte cartoon he once saw that showed how wi-fi and mobile computing had liberated people from the office desk. It showed a gloomy man in a striped suit sitting in the shade near a playground with an open laptop from which a chain ran to a shackle on his ankle. His laptop began to buzz and he felt a pang on his ankle from a tug on his phantom shackle.

'Hi, this is Colin speaking', said Colin once he had got his headset on and mouthpiece adjusted.

'Hi, Colin, Helena here. How are you settling in? You've already been with us two days, it must feel like a lifetime already!'

Helena had turned on her video and he could see the sun shining outside her office window on some trees at the edge of the forest, their branches weighed down with snow. Though perfectly logical, it still seemed surreal to him that it was two in the afternoon and minus five degrees in Brussels and Helena was working her normal day, while he was beginning the night shift, and had just turned on the air conditioning to break the oppressive heat. That morning, while he sweated on his way back from lunch, Helena might have been shovelling snow from her driveway.

'It does feel like a lot has been crammed into the two days. Well, almost two I suppose, considering today isn't really over yet.'

'Yes, well, there is that', admitted Helena, who knew exactly what he was driving at. 'Do you think it is manageable?' she asked, feeling that it was a rhetorical question. She was not expecting Colin to tell her that it was unworkable two days into the job, but did expect him to express some reservations now so that he could build up to something more down the road.

'Honestly, I'm not sure it is', said Colin, to a gasp that was just about audible at his end of the phone. 'I question the logic of hiring the role in Singapore when much of the IT work is going on in New York, you're based in Brussels and the end users are spread throughout the world. What was the reason behind the decision? If you don't mind me asking.'

'The main reason was that Mike felt that the role should be co-located with the sponsor, with him. The head of regional operations also wants to add seniority to the change team there. There should be strong opportunity for you to grow your career.'

'These were certainly some of the reasons that I thought of myself, but personal challenges aside, two people have already left on account of various problems, partly due to the fact that the role is located in the wrong place. This is bad for the project and it looks at least from the outside that we are willing to make the mistake a third time. This aside, from our combined experience we know that generally, and especially in crisis management, it is best to co-locate as much of the team as possible.'

'Let's come back to the issue of location difficulties later in the week, once you've had time to settle into a routine and have a better feel for your own time management', said Helena, though she seemed deep in thought as she replied.

'Well, before we do leave it I wanted to just run a couple of things by you in terms of management of my time. I have blocked my calendar to indicate that I am out of office between six and eight Singapore time so I can spend a couple of hours with my family. I'll be in the office until six but I'll take the night calls from home. I've also completely blocked out Friday evening. Do you think this can work?'

'Colin, you're free to do what you like to make it work. You can work on the moon for all I care. Your objective is not availability but delivery pure and simple. Now, coming back to the point you made earlier, do you think we are in crisis mode?' asked Helena, though she already knew the answer.

'I think that if we're not we probably should be. I would prefer to wait a few more days at least to discuss next steps', Colin began before Helena cut him off.

'I would appreciate it if you could provide Mike and me with an overview of your findings on Friday. The operations executive meet on Monday and I would like to ensure that we incorporate your views into the update. Does this work?'

'Yes, sure', replied Colin, doubtful that either Helena or Mike would be delighted with his assessment, whether it was presented on Friday or a month from now. He had a funny feeling, however, that everything he said was in line with expectations. That he had been on a prepared path from the time he stepped into the interview room and that while it seemed that he was making choices and observations and coming to conclusions of his own free will, the stimuli had been prearranged and he was following the expected path.

'Perfect. I will set the meeting up for Friday. Thanks for taking the time, Colin, we'll speak again in a little while at the change meeting.'

As her video disappeared he realised that he had not even started his own. For that matter he didn't know how to start it in the first place. He'd have to figure that one out; it was advantageous for meetings to at least seem face to face, even if it wasn't completely the same.

Before the meeting Colin had written down two desired outcomes. First, he wanted to make his working hours transparent and, second, to sow the seed that his review of the project would likely be unfavourable. Colin at least felt that he had been empowered to work on his own to his own timetable. While this was the least that he should have been able to expect, it was good to get it out of the way. While he had hoped to start work later in the morning, considering the late work he would be doing, it didn't seem possible, at least in the short term, especially considering the Friday deadline for his initial assessment. He wondered whether he would be going it alone on some of his conclusions or whether Serge would stand with him. He decided he would test the waters with him later that evening. He spent the time between calls catching up on emails that had been building up since he arrived and seemed to come in thick and fast from the beginning of the London day. He became so wrapped up in them that he jumped when the phone rang.

'Colin, you put a meeting in my calendar. I was expecting you to call. Is now a bad time?' Serge asked, sounding a bit put out.

Colin looked the clock on his computer. It was five past ten. 'Sorry, Serge, I'm not sure why the calendar didn't pop up to remind me of our meeting; I guess I need to change the settings, but I haven't got around to it yet.'

'Well, at least you got around to putting in some face time with me', replied Serge, who suddenly popped up on his screen. 'Hit the camera button and I'll get to see your ugly mug as well', he continued as Colin figured out how to get things working. 'This is almost as good as being in the same place except I'm at the office and if I were you I'd be sipping a beer at this time.'

'I'm not sure I'm going to get much of a chance for that in the evenings the way things are running.'

'All the more reason. Between you and me, any time I called Daniel he had a beer, felt it was his right if he was going to work into the night.'

'That might explain a lot. Problem with me is that I can't multitask. When I have a beer I have a beer and when I work I work. Each spoils the other for me. Tea usually gets me through. It may be boring, but it works.'

'Anyway, you set this meeting up; what was it you wanted to talk about?'

'Well, I was just wondering about the systems integration testing calls. It took us half the call yesterday to get through deciding if one of the problems raised was a defect or a change request', began Colin.

'Yeah, seriously, the business resources think they can have a free ride. They think they can introduce changes as they go along just because they realise that they want something that they didn't ask for in the first place. I mean, seriously, we've got to push back otherwise it's a free for all. We have a fixed-price contract with the vendor so every change request costs.'

'I get that and I agree that the stuff we actually want to change and code should be classified appropriately, but last night we talked for half an hour about something that was classified as low, which means we're not ever likely to even get to it. Do you think there's any way we could do it better so that we focus our time on the ones that matter?'

'Yeah, that was a serious waste of time. The IT teams are focused only on issues blocking us from moving forward with testing at the moment, and critical and high issues after that.'

'True, but besides the ones that you know about there are a whole pile that have not been classified', prompted Colin.

'What we should seriously be doing is agreeing the classi-fication of the issues against the criteria we agreed first, even before we decide whether it's a bug or a change request', replied Serge finally. 'That way when we have the conversa-tion about it being a change request or defect we'll be talking through the issues blocking testing and those that are critical to the business first.'

'Makes perfect sense to me, Serge, great idea. I'll follow your lead and support you on this if you want to raise it on the call later. It will make a big difference for defect resolution planning as well, as you will know what's in the queue to be fixed. The call should be less contentious as well, as it's been laid out pretty clinically what type of issue falls into which category.'

Colin was relieved that this had gone well. He had begun to lose the will to live during the call the night before. At least on the next call the attendees could move things forward somewhat. It was the first time he had heard about the vendor contract, though. He knew from previous discussions that the development had been outsourced to an IT solution provider and really only the IT management team were from Bank IB. This posed risks on its own but it was the first time he had heard that the contract was fixed price.

'You mentioned that the contract with IndoSign is fixed price', Colin began. 'Is this fixed price for delivery against the functional specifications?'

'Yes, exactly, it's against the functional specifications and for a specific time.'

'I don't understand', replied Colin, a little confused. In his experience, if a contract was for a fixed price for delivery against functional requirements agreed before pricing there would be no time limit. It seemed counter-intuitive.

'What's not to understand? Seriously, it's pretty standard. The contract is fixed against the functional specifications but there is agreement also that systems integration testing and user acceptance testing would only be supported for four weeks.'

'So you're saying that if the SIT or UAT goes longer than four weeks we have to pay more?'

'Yes, of course, that's in the contract', Serge responded, getting a little edgy; he could sense what was coming next. He had realised the flaw himself only recently but had said nothing, as he had been part of the negotiation team. 'This has to be expected', he continued defensively, 'otherwise the users could say they wanted to test indefinitely without signing off and the vendor would be bound to support if acceptance of the code was bound by the UAT sign-off.'

'The problem, though, is that the contract incentivises the vendor to deliver bad code because the longer they're fixing bugs the longer they're getting paid. It seems to me that the discussion regarding change request versus defect has become somewhat of a moot point now that we are past four weeks of SIT. If it is a change request we pay because it's over and above what was asked for in the functional specifications. If it is a defect it adds to the time of the SIT because IndoSign need to fix it and cash in as it does as well. What a great deal.'

The power of video chat over phone became painfully apparent as Colin looked at the screen and saw Serge silent and glowing red. He realised that he might have gone too far on the first call when he had been attempting to bring Serge onside. He knew he needed to change the subject, but most things on his list of topics to discuss were contentious, so he picked one that would allow Serge to vent further about business user behaviour.

'So how come the users are so involved in the SIT testing anyway? That's pretty unusual. Usually the IT team is solely responsible for it. Did they muscle their way in looking to get an early view of the system?' asked Colin, trying to show some understanding of the difficulties of working with assertive user groups and business sponsors.

'Well, actually it was IT who asked for their assistance to run some of the SIT test cases. We found that counter to your theory that the vendor would like testing to run for ever, the IT testers supplied by the vendor were not independent enough to test their own code so were passing everything. As we have little or no in-house testing capacity since the IT cuts were implemented last year, we asked the user community to lend a hand.'

'Okay, I understand', said Colin, deciding that he had probed enough for one day and had possibly found out too much to sleep soundly. 'Helena has asked me to provide my initial assessment of the programme status and what areas could be approved to get us back on track. She's put me under a bit of pressure and asked me to get something to her by Friday. I would like it to be a joint paper if you could help me. You know the project much better than I do and while there were, I am sure, perfectly legitimate reasons to make some of the decisions made, with hindsight, I wonder if there are some things you would change now. I think we're in a bit of a hole right now and if we can put something together and present it as a joint view I think it would be more impactful as a statement and set the ground for us to work together on the changes.'

'I'll give it some serious thought', replied Serge.

'Great. Thanks for that. Do you think you could give me something by the end of your day tomorrow? I will be spending my daytime on Thursday putting the pack together. We can discuss this during your Thursday morning. Just give me your thoughts, things you would do differently if you had a blank piece of paper. For example, the issues you have had on the IT side and where both business and IT could have worked better together. Maybe something on the vendor management side if you think it is appropriate.'

'Okay, talk to you in a bit', replied Serge, looking particularly disheartened.

Colin hung up and put his head in his hands.

6

Taking Project Control

It had been months since Colin had ridden his bike. Staring at his screen at one in the morning in his confined home office space, he had come to a conclusion. He would need to get more regular exercise and fresh air (a misnomer in Singapore) if he was to survive. His cycle to work was an ideal way of blowing away the cobwebs and taking in some beautiful scenery along the east coast of Singapore, through the park, along the seashore, under the coconut trees with the morning sun beating on his back. He loved the rhythmic churn of the pedals, like a mantra that emptied his mind. The downside was, of course, that he had to shower and change at work – it took less than five minutes on the bike to be wet through.

Although he had been up late again the night before, following his cycle and shower he could not help but feel refreshed and ready for more. He looked at his calendar and as expected it was pretty free in the morning. His first call was not until four in the afternoon, soon after London and Brussels got to the office. Jason wasn't in the office yet but he knew that he would begin to be less help to him as he moved towards his last day. Where Jason could help now was to provide him with some of the informal feedback and advice that he could comfortably give now that he was leaving the bank. That would be best discussed over lunch or a beer, though the evenings were pretty restricted. Suria, on the other hand, needed to be leveraged more. He thought of the RAID log discussion he had had with Jason the day before. The risks, assumptions, issues and dependencies in the log had not been updated for months. While it was nice to know the history, he wanted to start with a log that was at least up to date.

Colin opened up the RAID log by clicking on the link Jason had sent to him. It was in a standard spreadsheet format so the items could be filtered in different ways. As RAID templates went it was pretty good, in Colin's view.

The first column contained the item number so that the number could be referenced in discussions and seen on the printed page. The second column contained the item score, which was mathematically derived by multiplying numbers from two other columns – the probability that the issue would occur and the impact the issue would have on the project if it were to occur. These two numbers were in the range 0.1 at the lowest and 0.9 at the highest, so the product of the two would have a lowest score of 0.01 and a highest score of 0.81. An extreme example of a risk might be a meteorite hitting the building. The probability would be very low, indicated by 0.1, but the impact would be pretty high – 0.9. This would still leave a score of just 0.09. The options for selection were restricted so that a user could only select five options; 0.1, 0.3, 0.4, 0.6 and 0.9 in a scale that was almost Fibonaccian in nature. Simply put, the numbers represented probability and impact of very low, low, medium, high and very high. The item score was then used to drive the value of the 'handle' column describing how the issue would be handled. Anything less than or equal to 0.1 would be assigned the value 'monitor'; an event greater than 0.1 but less than 0.54 would be marked 'manage'; and anything higher than 0.54 'urgent'.

A second sheet in the workbook, in a separate tab, showed the probability and impact matrix in graphic format. The same tab showed an objective approach to impact assessment, describing the criteria that would have to be breached in cost, time, scope or quality for the impact to hit any of the representative numbers. In this scale, which Colin had to assume had been agreed with stakeholders at the initial meetings, a five to ten per cent increase in time was considered to be moderate, whereas ten to twenty per cent of cost increase was seen as moderate. If this was true it seemed that on-time delivery was more important to stakeholders than sticking to budget.

Going back to the list of items he saw that there was an action column with a choice of four action types – accept, avoid, mitigate or transfer – and a description of the action itself or how it was being executed. The RAID log also had columns for the date raised and date closed, who raised the item and who owned the item, the status (whether it was open or closed), as well as the item description itself. All in all it was a pretty useful template and the fields were populated to a high degree. The problem was that it was not up to date and that is where he needed Suria's assistance.

'Suria, do you have a moment?' he asked as he walked outside his office to Suria's desk. To Colin it seemed that either Suria was permanently in the office or had worked out how best to appear that he was.

'Yes, of course', replied Suria, getting up from his desk and following Colin into his office.

Colin sat at his desk and swivelled the monitor around so both he and Suria could see it. The RAID log was on the screen.

'I've been looking at the RAID log and I really like the template, it's well structured and logical. Unfortunately, that's going to be of little use to anyone unless it's up to date.'

'I think I know what's coming', said Suria with his eyebrows raised.

'Yes, I think you've guessed it. The old RAID items will be of interest to me as I get to grips with the project and I want to go back and see some of the history that got us here but until I am on top of what is going on today I need to be able to filter by the items that are open and urgent for a start. Could you please own the log and ensure that it is brought up to date as soon as possible?'

'No problem, though I'm not sure I'll have a view on all issues.'

'That's fine', replied Colin, 'I didn't think that you would have. If you can take a first stab at closing the items that are already in there that are from another life, that would be a start. Then perhaps you could update the items you know are still open by following up with the owners to get the most up-to-date view and finally work with Serge and Jason to add any items that should be there today that are not.'

'Do we need to update all of the issues being found in testing in here too?'

'No, that's not the point. This is the project RAID log and not a defect tracker. With regard to the SIT I would expect to see an issue relating to the number of defects being raised, maybe an issue on the environment stability, an issue regarding the number of change requests being raised – all items that would be considered project issues rather than testing issues.'

'Okay, that's pretty clear. I'll get on to that straightaway. Let me know if you need anything else.'

'Thanks, Suria, there's nothing else for now. I could ask, though, that you absolutely scrape the bottom of the barrel in terms of what you put into the log. I would rather see a hundred things too many than one too few.'

When Suria left Colin somehow felt confident that he would get what he was asking for and that would not only help his understanding of the areas of concern but would also feed into the assessment that he needed to prepare in the following few days. He then turned his attention to the stakeholder matrix. Once again it was a useful document in spreadsheet format. He liked this from a structure perspective, as it was easy to manipulate, filter and view in different ways, as long as it was used correctly. Colin filtered by 'Singapore' to find all the stakeholders based there. As he did so he also saw values for 'SG', 'SIN', SING' and 'SPORE'. He also saw 'New York', 'US' and 'NY'. Looking through the spreadsheet there were a lot of things that could be cleaned up. For it to be useful it should be standardised.

'Daisy, are you busy?' he asked as he approached her desk.

'That's a trick question if ever I heard one', Daisy replied cryptically. 'I can make time if there's something you need me to do.'

Colin hadn't thought about what had been occupying Daisy's time, but now that she had drawn attention to it he did wonder. It was something he would ask Jason about, if ever he came in.

'How good are you with spreadsheets?' he asked, gesturing for Daisy to follow him into his office.

'I know my way around. I'm pretty good as long as you are not asking me to write macros or create complicated pivots.'

'No, I'm not looking for anything like that.'

Colin turned his screen around again and showed Daisy the stakeholder spreadsheet. 'All I really want is to get this cleaned up and standardised. If you could put two-character standard ISO codes for the countries where people are located and …'

'ISO codes?' Daisy interrupted.

'Just the standard codes, like UK for United Kingdom, IE for Ireland, SG for Singapore, you know what I mean.'

'Yeah, sure. Why didn't you just say that? Though you do know we don't even have an office in Ireland, right? Do you have banks there?'

'Anyway, the codes for the countries', Colin continued, ignoring Daisy's questions, 'and standardise departments as well. It's pretty useful to be able to group the list in this way as well. Besides this it looks like the information is generally out of date. People's roles and responsibilities need to be updated. The people who are no longer working on the project should be removed. No, actually, leave them in there but please grey them out; then I'll understand who people are talking about if they refer to them.'

'Anything else?' asked Daisy while Colin tried to figure out if she was trying to get as much instruction as possible to help her with her task or if she just wanted to get out of his office and back to whatever she was doing.

'I think you can work out the rest. I'd just like the stakeholder list to be more useful. Do you think you can manage this?'

'I'll do my best', she sang as she walked out of the door, almost bumping into Jason as he came in.

'Come in, come in', Colin said, feeling that although his office felt a bit like a train station he was making some progress in moving along the things he needed to.

'We got through a pile of issues last night', Jason said. 'With any luck the fixes will be in the test environment by Friday.'

'Good morning to you, too', Colin said, smiling. 'Yes, you're right, we got through a lot last night but I think we could have done even more. The previous night we spent time arguing whether or not a "low" defect was a change request, and that was obviously a waste of time. Last night there was too much discussion on whether the issue was critical or high or medium when there are so many issues that there are enough critical and high issues to last the development team weeks and these simply have to be done.'

'Yes, but the point is that if the development team can change the issue from high to medium it's one less issue that they have to focus on', replied Jason.

'I think there may be an easier way of doing this', continued Colin. 'Let's say there are three hundred open items and, though we don't know it, there are one hundred critical, one hundred high and one hundred medium-severity problems. If we ask the users and SMEs to force rank them themselves with no IT involvement we are already on to a winner. While it could be argued that the bias of the user is to get everything done and therefore will argue that something is a critical issue even if it is not, they would be doing themselves a disservice if they were to prioritise an issue that was not so important over a critical item', suggested Colin.

'I could also talk to them and ask if they could do this during the day here in Singapore so we would not even need to have the prioritisation call', added Jason.

'Exactly', replied Colin. 'We should also get someone independent to make a first pass at checking categorisation of items as change requests or defects. There are going to be obvious change requests and obvious defects and then some in a grey area. For the obvious change requests, the functional specification area where the function is described should be written into the defect tracker. The obvious change requests should be prioritised by the users in a forced ranked list, the same as the defects, so that these can be worked through top to bottom. If we get to items that we all might consider low priority, it is then we need to have some more serious discussions.'

In his mind's eye Colin could already see some space opening up in his calendar. 'Once we have this in place we can move the defects calls to twice a week. This should then be focused on tracking issues from the time they are raised to when they get delivered, providing business clarification and answering questions to help IT deliver. We could then focus on actual delivery through ageing metrics and the like.'

'Patricia Ng is the lead subject matter expert in the operations team; I'll set some time in her calendar today to go through the new procedure with her', Jason said as he began to walk back to his desk.

'Perfect. Do you think Daisy could sort the obvious defects from the change requests and map back the functional specification area in the defect tracker?'

'I'll go and ask her to do that as well and then come back to talk to you about the business requirements documents and things you asked about in the email you sent last night.'

'Thanks', said Colin, only just remembering that he actually had sent an email the night before. It had been pretty late and as the teams were arguing over issue criticality, rather than intervening and getting in the middle of it he had begun to answer some emails. It was one of those nights when he asked himself if it was all really worthwhile, but it all looked better after a night's sleep. He firmly believed that sleep could change the lens through which life is viewed.

When Jason did come back he had the detailed project plan open on his screen. 'Why are we doing this project?' Colin asked as simply as if he had asked the time.

'To save money for the bank by automating the process', Jason replied

Colin was about to reply but changed his mind. There was no need to educate Jason at this late stage but it was obvious from the fact that the right answer did not roll off Jason's tongue that communicating the project goal would need to be addressed.

'Could you walk me through the plan?'

'I can, in that I remember going through it with Daniel some time ago, but it has not been updated in a while.'

Colin had seen that it had been updated six months ago but there was no point in bringing that up.

'The project plan has a fairly standard software development life cycle or SDLC structure. It has a waterfall approach so, as you know, one thing gets done after the other in succession and with a higher quality required on each of the phased deliveries.'

Colin couldn't help smiling. If higher quality meant scratching out things in the FRDs and handing them over in that way it was an interesting view on quality.

'I can see you think that's a bit funny but it was run that way until we shifted tack. Mike is pretty action-oriented and wanted to see results quickly, so shortcuts were taken. He and Daniel were at loggerheads much of the time as Daniel was a true blue, by the book, PRINCE2-certified, structured project manager. If it didn't say it in the PRINCE2 guide then there was nothing to talk about. Mike, on the other hand, had no time for Daniel's talk of project artefacts and the like. I remember being part of a discussion where Mike asked him if he thought he was an archaeologist with all his talk of artefacts. He said that if he didn't get a move on and deliver an archaeologist would be digging up his artefacts before a collateral trade was processed on the system.'

'Fair enough', said Colin, who was realising he would need ammunition for the discussion he was going to have with Mike and Helena on Friday.

'So yes, in the beginning, when things were being done by the book the target operating model was written with detailed as-is analysis and a good view of the future state with associated roles and responsibilities. The business requirements document was written using the TOM as a guide with every requirement mapped back to an area in the TOM. The functional requirements document was written so that it broke the requirements in the BRD into functions that could be coded into the system and these were in turn mapped back to those BRD areas against which they were written. You can see each of these items in the plan with dates against them, people responsible and the associated dependencies.'

As Colin looked at the plan he could see it all laid out and well structured, and the tasks even seemed to have been done on time. It was then that the percentage complete on the tasks changed from a hundred per cent to a mix and match of completion estimates.

'The tech specs were never written against the functional requirements document, were they?' asked Colin. 'It looks like it's here that things began to go wrong.'

'Exactly. Before the IT team wrote the technical specifications it was realised that the project was heading in the wrong direction. Mike had no tolerance for taking things back to the start again so he asked that the functional specifications be changed. We had a series of meetings where he and some of his team dictated how they saw changes to be made and the FRDs were marked up and changed based on this. The technical specifications were written based on the marked-up document and the coding was based on this tech spec.'

'And the test cases for SIT were written using the marked-up FRDs', Colin finished.

'Yes, that's about the size of it. You don't see any of this in the plan as the plan was written based on the original way of doing things. I mean we followed a lot of the same things but not exactly as it was laid out.'

'Well, obviously the code was written, the code was unit tested, run through QA and then put in SIT, where it is now languishing.'

'Yes, again right', replied Jason, 'but in this case some of the coding would have been done by different teams in different systems as the future state changed.'

'What do you mean?' asked Colin.

'Well, the changes were pretty fundamental. The original requirements had collateral bookings being made by the processing team but the new future state bookings are done by the front office traders in their front office systems, for example. In this case the development needs to happen in a different system by a different team.'

'So this plan is pretty useless, then', said Colin, shaking his head.

'Not completely, as much of the go-live tasks can be re-used and some of the estimations, team effort and work packages are the same, but yes, you're right, it needs a lot of rework.'

'Was there ever a discussion on an agile approach to the software development?'

'It was something Daniel brought up. The way he explained it is that the software would be developed in iterations and more or less built through working with a delivery, asking for changes, getting these delivered and iterating until the requested changes were trivial.'

'Did he get far in the discussion?'

'Not really. The original sponsor liked the idea of getting something quickly that he could get his users on to but it was thought that something so big and so complex needed a more robust approach. Roberto Giovanni is pretty old school and dismissed the idea outright. He began to rant that everyone was crazy if they thought his team would begin to build something from a conversation or the back of a beer mat. Helena, probably correctly, wondered if we had the maturity to take the approach and if there could be the level of collaboration between teams to make this work. Looking back now I wonder whether she was looking for Roberto to defend his team's working maturity and ability to work collaboratively but he either missed it, ignored it because he had no interest in the method, or maybe he just agreed.'

When Jason left for the meeting he had scheduled earlier Colin began to take stock of the situation. He had a deadline to meet on Friday but he still wanted to get some foundation documentation in place that could focus his thoughts on what needed to be done. He had that afternoon, Thursday and Friday morning to prepare for his meeting with Helena and Mike. To be ready he wanted to ensure he had a rounded view of the issues. To do this he would use the input from Serge, and Suria was updating the RAID log with his and others' input. He also wanted to update the governance and communications deck so that he could show the organisation that was in place as well as the gaps he saw in the structure. He felt he needed a scope statement, to rework the charter and objectives, and to have some view on the cost. Before he forgot, he wrote a quick email to Serge asking for the budget and forecast information. Besides this, as a base he would need to present the project issues in a structured way and make convincing arguments for some pretty fundamental changes. So all in all he felt he had some fun days ahead.

7

Governance and Budget Management

The project will functionalise the collateral process, align roles and responsibilities to emerging regulations, reduce booking and processing risk, and increase automation.

Colin thought that this was as good a description of the project objective that he had heard and at least it was something that could be discussed in open forum. It was easy to understand, something people should be able to get behind and something all requirements could be judged against. It was also about as succinct as he could make it. He read it a number of times and committed it to memory. He would use it, with little variation, over and over again in the coming months in steering committees, working groups and even elevator conversations. Irrespective of who asked the question or who was answering it, the idea would be that the outcome would be the same. In his mind only philosophies that were universally understood and accepted became self-fulfilling. It would also mean that any change request, new requirement, scope change or new idea could be judged against a simple common objective. If it aligned there was a discussion to be had; if it did not there was nothing to talk about.

He began the new project charter with this stated as the project objective. He then laid out individual bullets under the statement to list concrete delivery objectives, which included replacement of MargCalc, the legacy margining calculation tool; implementation of a new collateral processing tool; and delivery of standardised processes aligned to the target operating model. Taking these objectives, he then wrote the opportunity statement and background to outline why the current state, without the delivery of these objectives, was sub-optimal and put this before the objective. As if writing a story, he then had the problem statement and the proposed solution.

Having completed the qualitative side of the project's raison d'être he then moved to the quantitative side, reusing much of the information that had been provided in the initial business case, including the cost savings from decommissioning legacy systems. He didn't add the headcount savings he expected from the new approach because, first, these had not been agreed, and second, he was not pitching a new business case to get funds but only revamping the charter for reference and alignment. While leaving it in might have been a demotivating factor for the operations team supporting the implementation, he would not have omitted the benefit for this reason alone. He left the scope statement as it was written along with the key issues and risks, which were pretty generic. Last, he tweaked some of the organisational information. He did not touch the schedule as it was documented as it would require some further analysis before it could be updated.

Happy with this as a start he opened up the organisation chart. It showed himself as the project manager of the project reporting to the steering committee. It showed Jason as the stream lead for over the counter or OTC trades, and Suria as business analyst reporting to Jason. There were two other stream lead roles, but both boxes had 'TBD' entered instead of a lead role. It seemed strange to Colin that there was a stream lead for OTC and a project manager for the project overall, but it looked as though no other stream had been initiated. From what he had seen so far, no other stream should be initiated before this one was sorted out. Had he thought it possible to run simultaneous streams he would have put Suria in one of the stream lead roles. He knew Suria wanted the role badly and would work for it. He believed also that by putting him in that role Suria would be willing to 'double hat' as the business analyst until a new one was hired and would support the new hire until he or she was up to speed. Though this was all true, and it would have been easier to delegate some of his own responsibilities, he felt that until the project was back on track he needed to be completely focused as the project manager for the project and delivery of this stream.

He redrew the organisation chart to show the organisation for this delivery phase only, which would deliver the foundation of the collateral system and the OTC release, with himself as the project manager and Suria as the lead business analyst. He then added as lead a subject matter expert from the operations collateral management unit. Though it might have been unusual at Bank IB to have the SMEs with other roles in the operations area shown in the organisation chart, Colin felt that this practice of omission was demotivating for the staff working in those roles and led to ambiguity over their responsibilities and time commitments. A name on the chart put their skin in the game. The SMEs were particularly important as they, and their immediate line manager, would have to agree to the matrix structure and the time commitment if it was transparent in this way.

He then added a target operating model lead and a testing lead, as his own direct reports. This created a flat, focused organisation structure. He considered adding a further role for the design authority but instead decided that the TOM lead, if selected properly, could also fulfil this role and represent the project at any design review boards.

Finally, he added a slide under the organisation chart and built out the descriptions of the roles and responsibilities of everyone in the chart. Putting them down on paper would either make those accountable and responsible pretty uncomfortable or put them at ease. Either outcome was equally valuable: being at ease with the description would mean that everyone understood what was expected of the role and was in agreement with it; discomfort meant that an issue had been festering behind the scenes and causing a drag on progress. Shedding light on it would help smooth the way.

Colin next turned his attention to the project governance. He had gone through this briefly on his first day and was glad to see the types of meeting that he would expect to see. There was a steering group and a working group; but on looking more closely at these, once again the names of the attendees seemed to be out of date. Either this was just a documentation issue or – more likely, going by his experience so far – these meetings were agreed in principle but in practice were not in place. Colin looked out of his door and that saw that Jason was back at his desk.

'Do you have a minute, Jason?'

'I was just leaving for lunch', Jason began, 'I have an appointment.'

'That's okay', replied Colin, 'I really mean just a minute. I was going through the governance papers and went to the site that Daisy forwarded to me. The last steering committee minutes I can find are from July. Is this because ...'

'... there has been no steering committee since July?' Jason said, completing Colin's question. 'That's right. The August STC was cancelled due to unavailability because of the summer holiday period and then the September STC began but ended rather abruptly, as I explained earlier, with no small degree of drama. There were no minutes. Some say there may have been an oral request, in confidence, that the minutes not be recorded, but I couldn't possibly comment on such fruitless speculation', he said with a sly smile.

'And since then?' Colin asked.

'There are no minutes as there were no meetings since then. I'm late, so give me a shout as soon as I get back if you need anything.'

With that Jason left for lunch and Colin felt some kind of pang in his gut that could have been hunger. He might have been somewhat stunned that there had been no formal governance oversight of the project in seven months, but he had expected this. It was also clear to see that Jason had now more or less completely checked out of his role. He was just going through the motions. That too was no surprise. Sitting back at his desk Colin updated the steering group members list as far as he could from his knowledge so far and the stakeholder matrix that was available. He then reviewed the objectives of the steering group, which were pretty stand-ard. The steering group was there to provide guidance and direction. It was chaired by the sponsor, administered by the project manager and together with these two individu-als shared accountability for the budget, scope and delivery of the business benefits. It also acted as an escalation point for key issues and risks. Colin decided that the next meeting would need to be scheduled, with Helena and Mike's approval, as soon as possible.

There was no mention of a design review board so he added this to the pack, but scheduled this as a quarterly rather than monthly meeting. The objective of the design review board would be to validate IT and business architectural decisions, to approve the target operating model and the target end state IT architecture. The board should provide independ-ent assessment and verification that the architecture and operating model were in line with the strategic bank-wide end state. It would need to be a cross-divisional group and he would need to get suggestions for the participants from Helena.

In the meantime he acknowledged that the pain in his gut was at least partially due to hunger and he would have to do something about it. On this Wednesday, his third day on the project, he felt a routine was developing and he now saw lunch as the end of one third of his day. Dinner with Clara would be two-thirds of the day gone, and that was when he realised the reason for his greater feeling of unease.

As he had been going through the project documentation he had been scraping at the surface, uncovering many good reasons why the project was in trouble and beginning to formulate ways to remediate the issues. But it was as if while scraping away the grime that was hiding the problems to be addressed he had been avoiding a key mitigating action. He had already said it out loud, but only half-heartedly, not realising the implications for him personally. Had he been asked to look at the project for a day as an independent assessor he would have recommended in the first hour that the project team be co-located. He had been asking himself repeatedly why the role had been hired in Singapore but had never asked if interviews had been conducted elsewhere. Every one of his interviewers knew the project, its history and the demands of running it from Singapore. They knew he would be sitting here now measuring his days in thirds. Perhaps he was hired in spite of his location rather than because of it. It suddenly dawned on him that somehow there was an expectation that he would move from Singapore. He put his head in his hands as memories of the interview with Helena came flooding back. The small talk at the beginning may in fact have been the heart of the interview. In a subtle, conversational and casual way she had built up a complete picture of his connections to Singapore, his views on the advantages and challenges of expat living and his time horizon for staying in Asia. In answering her questions he had surprised himself by the answers he had at the ready, that he could provide with confidence, for questions he had so far avoided asking himself. Though he might have thought about some of them, he had never articulated them consistently and coherently. He himself learned of his own views during that conversation, but he had completely missed its importance. He got up from his desk and walked out of the office, his mind working furiously at this realisation and what it meant. He and Clara had talked about moving before. Every time they both agreed that they would stay another year. That had been going on for more than six years. They both knew in their hearts, though, that it would take an event, a big push or a strong pull for them to make a decision to change. Not wanting to stray far in the midday heat on his own, he ended up once again getting a sandwich and taking it back to his desk, where he found himself dialling his home number.

'Hi, it's me, how's your day going?'

'Not bad. Marie's just gone down for her nap; she was no trouble today. Is everything all right?'

'Yeah, I just grabbed a sandwich and thought I'd give you a call.'

'We're leaving, aren't we?' Clara suddenly said.

'I don't know, but I'm getting that feeling', replied Colin as if it was the most normal thing in the world for Clara to have read his mind or for them to have come to the same conclusion simultaneously. Clara would describe such a meeting of minds as a connection between them and an ability to listen and articulate her own intuition. Colin viewed it as subconscious observation of all of the pieces of a puzzle as they come together, a picture emerging, seemingly miraculously, with the last piece. But he liked her version better and he knew that either way it only worked because they were close, open and equal partners in everything.

'It might be time. Do you know when or where?'

'I haven't even got to that in my head yet. I think Brussels would make most sense, but that's just my gut right now. Let's take it a step at a time. I'll know more by Friday.'

'I'll miss Singapore. This is likely to be tougher than we thought, but we'll get through it just like everything else.'

Colin felt unburdened. Clara was not an unquestioning trailing spouse; she was a partner who walked in step with Colin and would sometimes lead their thought processes. She believed in a fate that drove people in the right direction. If they were to move from Singapore Colin's job might be the catalyst, but the reason could just as well have been related to where she needed to be. Her reaction showed that she had thought deeply, if subconsciously, about the impacts and potential outcomes and had come to an independent decision that if the option were to present itself then it would be the right time. Knowing that Clara was open to relocation as an outcome allowed Colin to focus on the options as they related to the project.

After his call with Clara he began to scribble while munching on his tandoori chicken sandwich, which was at least a little better than the chewing-gum beef he had had on the last occasion. His scribbles were lists of names and locations, the primary stakeholders at this stage of the project and who he thought would become more important in later stages. He started putting symbols – stars, circles or triangles – against names as categories came into his head of reasons to interact with stakeholders in a particular location. He added more symbols for phases of the project and where proximity would mean the most at those times. He did none of this in any structured way, but began to see the pattern emerge, as he had expected, around Brussels. He cursed the lack of attention he had paid in French classes at school. He decided to stop looking at this for now, as he knew it could become a big distraction. Knowing that it was likely that moving would be the right thing to do was enough for now. He would structure his thoughts about it all before Friday, but for now he would let it work through in his subconscious and be fed by his project analysis.

Colin moved his attention to the budget. Serge had sent him the budget, actuals and forecast, as he had requested, by email. There was a spreadsheet with budget versus actuals for 2009 and, as Mike had said, it looked at first glance as though the project had come in a million under budget for the full year. Actual costs had already been put in for January and these were in line with the forecast. The problem was that Colin knew that the project was running over budget. The problem with the finance statements was that they took no deliveries into account. A budget for running a line control function could be viewed 'straight' in terms of budget, actual spend and forecast, but a project budget needed to take account of the value earned by the money spent. While a project that spent one million against a budget of one million for a given year might seem at first glance to have hit the budget on the nose, if the project team squandered the lot in the local bar and delivered nothing, it was in reality a million over budget.

Though Colin was not a great fan of earned value analysis, or EVA, as a tool to use on an ongoing basis, it was a useful tool to explain in more detail the health of a project in progress. Using the data Serge had sent him, the schedule as it was originally baselined and what he knew of what had been completed to date, Colin spent the rest of the afternoon building up a picture of the cost profile of the project. Every calculation he documented reinforced what he already knew. While only five million had been spent in 2009 against a budget of seven million, the project had delivered only about half of the items that were budgeted. In other words, the project had delivered things that were estimated to cost 3.5 million to deliver within that year, but had paid five million to get them delivered. Viewed in this way, things looked somewhat less positive. Using estimations of budget associated with each of the deliveries, he plotted a curve representing the budgeted spend according to the way the project was originally scheduled. Comparing this budgeted cost of work scheduled, or BCWS, to the budgeted cost of the work performed (BCWP) showed graphically what the schedule variance looked like. He then added a further curve for the actual cost of the work performed (ACWP). This showed the cost variance independent of the schedule variance. Using some standard EVA formulae he extrapolated out this ACWP line to forecast completion schedule and cost. Finally he added the results of the earned value management formulae to the same page as the graph so that everything could be viewed on one page. The formulae included performance indicators for cost and schedule as well as the independent estimate at completion. While the figures reinforced what he already knew, he felt it was important to perform and present the due diligence behind what could be perceived as an ill-informed statement that the project was over budget and behind schedule. Helena and Mike might care less about the budget, or they might already know the situation, but Colin preferred to provide a complete picture rather than make assumptions about what was needed. It would be up to Mike and Helena to decide what to do with the information.

8

Politics

The morning seemed fresher and clearer than usual as Colin cycled to the office. Along the beach a pleasant onshore breeze swayed the coconut trees along the East Coast Parkway. It seemed to blow from the orange sun rising fast over Bintan, one of the many islands of Indonesia, which could be seen unusually clearly across the Straits. It was as if Singapore was teasing him with her beauty and what he would likely leave behind.

His calls had finished by eleven the night before so he had had a longer sleep than on his first two nights. He had been hoping to get a first view of the email Serge had agreed to send, covering the project learning points, before he went to bed. It would have been worthwhile to discuss the content and have any questions answered before he incorporated the information into his presentation material. Unfortunately nothing was sent through and though Serge was on the calls it seemed that he disappeared into thin air immediately afterwards and could not be reached by phone or email. Colin thought about how much easier it would have been to be able to wander into the office next door. Even being in the same country would have helped.

He cycled past the Laguna Country Club, where middle-aged men in luminous trousers were playing an early round of golf, and managed to hit fifty kilometres an hour pushing his pedals hard from the Tanah Merah Flyover onto Xilin Avenue. It was not that he needed a thrill in the morning – getting ahead of the traffic at breakneck speed in the middle of the road, where he could be seen, was preferable to construction trucks flitting past him within arm's reach when he went slowly. Singaporeans didn't cycle much on the road and drivers were not used to bicycle traffic. The traditional karung guni, or rag-and-bone men, solved the problem by cycling in the middle of the road against the oncoming traffic, but Colin couldn't bring himself to try this novel approach.

By the time he had showered and booted up his computer he had already resigned himself to the prospect of further complications in Serge's email. If Serge had, as he suspected, been avoiding him, it was unlikely that any good could come of it. He was already disappointed that he had failed to connect with Serge in a way that could form the basis of a partnership for delivery throughout the life of the project. He felt that once again he had rushed in, as he usually did, to find answers and resolve problems rather than first building relationships. This, not any of his set interview pieces, was his true weakness, he felt, and something that did make a material difference to how quickly he could get things done. While he enjoyed the feeling of progress as he ploughed through the work himself, project work was about leveraging the whole team to get through the work more quickly and more efficiently. People were generally more amenable and motivated to work with someone with whom they had some kind of relationship. All that said, he could not be too hard on himself; he had been on the job for only three days and had already been tasked with presenting a project assessment. When finally his email inbox popped up he realised it was not the content of Serge's email that was the problem, it was the lack of any communication at all from him. Once again he was on his own and once again the fact that he had no recourse but to wait for twelve hours to discuss this gave further weight, as if he needed any, that all of the core team needed to be co-located.

Colin closed his door as the penny finally dropped. He was the auditor and the executioner. Independent from the project as it had been run, independent from the IT team who had been part of the delivery so far, and someone who had probably been hired because he could cut to the chase. Serge had not replied because what he would write would be damning of both his own actions thus far and those of his superiors. He had decided to stand on the outside rather than move to the inside of a change that was inevitably going to happen. Colin felt that, unfortunately, this would have to be part of the assessment he presented and although his mind had until now been on the relationships that he would need to build with the IT team, he felt that it was already more about bringing about an understanding that fundamental change needed to take place to get this project over the line.

Colin began his story. It needed to be a story because, like projects, stories have a beginning, a middle and an end. If the reader is lucky they will even have some kind of arc, a struggle, a climax and a dénouement, just like a project should have.

On the first slide Colin succinctly laid out history and context. It described how a project was initiated to improve the way collateral was processed in Bank Investissement Belgique, to reduce booking and processing risk, and to increase automation. Following the realisation that processes within the collateral world were similar to other functional processes and that regulation was driving further segregation of duties between the front, middle and back offices, the project direction changed. The sponsorship and some of the team changed at the same time. Following on from this the project continued under different guidance with the objective being to functionalise the collateral process, align roles and responsibilities to emerging regulations, reduce booking and processing risk, and increase automation.

The next slides outlined the various issues that Colin had observed and his proposed remediation. Though needing to operate at a global level to ensure consistent processes, the team was distributed unnecessarily across the world. IT leadership was centred in New York and business project management, PMO and business analysis were all based in Singapore, as was the sponsor of the project. Operations change leadership and some of the core users were based in Brussels. The vendor, IndoSign, was based in Bangalore in India. While it could be expected that there would be peaks and troughs in the project, the distribution of the project team meant that burnout was likely and evident even during the slower project phases. The distribution had also led to relationships not conducive to expedient delivery, lack of cohesion, slow communication and views that were over-regionalised, leading to behaviour bordering on territoriality. The painfully obviously solution to this was to co-locate the core project team. That included at least the IT delivery manager, business project manager, stream leads and subject matter experts. It also extended to the vendor, but this was dealt with in a separate point.

The project was built on shaky foundation. All core documentation was inadequate. The target operating model (TOM) was written to reflect an ideal that was past its sell-by date. It was not detailed enough to be useful in understanding the process flows and ensuring that they were implemented correctly and consistently. The business requirements documents were not written against a detailed TOM, and were inadequate to even effectively differentiate change requests from genuine defects. The functional specifications, and therefore the technical specifications, lacked depth or quality by virtue of the fact they were written on a layer of documents that lacked quality, and furthermore by depth, quality and relevance issues of their own. It had become obvious, through sitting on the various calls and reading the IT-driven documentation, that the IT vendor resources lacked the basic understanding of the business area to implement the users' requirements. The sum of these problems meant that the users really didn't know what they were testing and the development vendor didn't understand what it was meant to code in the first place.

What could be seen on a day-to-day basis was that the process of waterfall software development life cycle (SDLC) had been discarded in favour of a quasi-agile approach. Simply put, the users would test something, find it was not what they wanted and explain on the phone what they in fact did want. The vendor would then attempt to change the system accordingly, with little understanding of the business or process. The teams, vendor and project were not set up to manage agile development in any kind of effective way and in the end everyone ended up chasing their own tails and stepping on top of each other. Had the vendor had some expertise in the subject matter or been competent enough to leverage the users' knowledge more effectively, things could have progressed more quickly, but this simply was not the case. Had they been asked to develop shoes with laces they would have needed the instruction to include eyelets to lace the shoes.

The first point of remediation was to stop. Stop everything that was being done to test and develop a system with no foundation. The second step was to remediate the underlying causes of the problems.

The vendor itself and the contract – or lack thereof – was also exacerbating the problem. They were, unfortunately, motivated and incentivised to get things wrong. Every day of extra testing was more money in the coffers. Every issue found or change request added was money on the bottom line. The defect rate in the code was extremely high, even for this type of project. The turnaround time for fixing defects raised was far slower than should have been expected. When fixes were released for retest the failure rate during retest was more than half of the fixes implemented. Colin included the actual statistics he was able to pull from the test tracking tool and included industry averages and statistics that were available from other Bank IB projects he had found on the intranet. Everything pointed to very poor performance from the vendor, which may have been taking advantage of a contract that was very much in its favour. The vendor had to go and a new vendor would need to take its place. The new vendor would need to have a track record for this type of development, be contracted at more favourable terms, develop the code in the same time zone as the core project team and co-locate key people with the core project team.

The project was not staffed effectively. Collin added to the pack the governance slide that he had prepared earlier and listed the open roles and why they were needed. He then added what he called his SWAT team; a team of people who would be required very short term to lay the foundations by reusing what was available and applying industry standards, rigour and best practice methodology. He suggested a four-person team supplemented by two business requirements document writers to complete the TOM urgently. He suggested that this team come from a specialist firm familiar with collateral solutions implemented at similar organisations. In this way there would be some off-the-shelf industry-standardised processes they could use which would reduce the time and effort that would have been needed to reinvent the wheel. They would also be able to keep the Bank IB SMEs in check in terms of their requests that might bring the bank in the wrong direction and sort out the nice-to-have items from the critical delivery components.

Given the right remit and access, Colin believed that the TOM issue could be resolved within two months. If done iteratively from concepts and design statements in a first phase down to the detailed process flows and related sub-process flows in later stages, the early phases could be used effectively as basis for the business requirements documents. On this basis the BRDs could begin within about two weeks of the TOM work starting, initially using the two BRD writers who had supplemented the TOM team and adding a further two people to support the work. The original two people would already be familiar with the core flows, key SMEs and the project in general, and this once again should expedite the effort. If these resources were to work hand in glove with the TOM team they would be able to run this effort in parallel and could finish, he estimated, in about two months, if they were dedicated to this work only and given the required support. It was an added advantage that the SMEs had seen something of the system and process flows already built; this meant that the conversations around the TOM, BRDs and process flows would be based on practical experience rather than on the abstract and theoretical view they would normally have had if the process had started with a blank page.

The project was significantly over budget. Colin used the earned value analysis he had undertaken earlier and pulled these charts and figures into the presentation. He then added his SWAT team estimates, bumping his initial two-month estimate to three full months to cover the worst-case scenario he believed possible. It was by no means the bottom-up estimating he would have preferred to undertake, but it felt right; and he had until the next day to present something that made sense. He had ascertained from the vendor contract sent by Serge that though IndoSign were fleecing Bank IB they had no notice period built into the contract. On that basis, sending a note for them to stop work immediately would save money from that very date. Colin built this into the estimates as well as a two-month reprieve from paying any vendor costs while a vendor selection process could take place. When looked on in this way the run rate of the project would actually reduce for two months rather than increase, even accounting for the SWAT team of specialist vendor resources. If the project had been running to schedule it could have been argued that in the proposed two or three months, rework could have led the end date to move by at least the same period. Given that there was no end in sight to the current testing phase, Colin could argue that this pause could actually bring the implementation date closer than other options. Though he would have liked to have a projected go-live date based on his new plan, he knew that this would be pure speculation: he did not know how much of the code would need to be rewritten, how much would need to be added or how many of the process flows developed were close to what would be a new TOM. He also knew that the new vendor would have a view and he could not commit to anything unless he first had everyone's buy-in. What he could add was a three-month target date to present this plan and proposed budget from the time the go-ahead was given to proceed.

He reviewed his slides again from the perspective of the story he was telling and the message he wanted to get across. He had provided a background to the situation in the initial slides. He then outlined the problems of team disbursement, inadequate foundation documentation, vendor expertise, alignment, and contracting, staffing and budget, as well as his proposed remediation in these areas. Colin documented the next steps as a decision by the sponsor and head of change to proceed along this path, with agreement from IT. If this was agreed then he would formulate a note to all stakeholders that the programme would be re-planned with the first phase set out at the next steering committee meeting. He would then complete an indicative plan and the key milestones that needed to be delivered over the next three months and discuss this, in advance of the STC, with all the STC members. He knew he would need to discuss the proposal with IT before meeting with Mike and Helena, even if Serge had declined to be a part of it. His co-location proposal effectively either removed Serge from his role in the programme or imposed a move from New York to Brussels. Despite Serge's wanderlust, he knew this would not go down well. He checked his calendar and invited Serge to an 11 p.m. meeting. He did not send him the discussion deck; he thought it better to first talk about it with Serge – this type of news would be better coming in a setting as close to face to face as possible.

Colin spent the rest of the time before lunch getting the presentation deck right. While he did want it to look professional, most of his time was spent getting the facts and figures in order rather than polishing it. He checked back over the vendor contract, revisited the earned value analysis numbers and the testing statistics. He also reviewed the newly updated risks, assumptions, issues and dependencies, or RAID, log that Suria had sent him. It was great to have this up to date, but in the end he still felt that it gave symptoms of the problems rather than a description of the underlying causes. Just to make sure, he read every open item, mentally relating everything back to the causes requiring remediation that he had documented in the presentation pack. Viewing each of the problems and proposed solutions in isolation, the individual remediation proposals made perfect sense. He wasn't oblivious, however, to the fact that when looked at cumulatively the problems were damning for those with delivery accountability and that the remediation was dramatic to say the least. He wondered how Helena and Mike would view his assessment and remediation proposal. As he pondered, Jason came to the glass door, knocked and opened it just enough to talk through the crack.

'Hi, Colin, you've had yourself locked up here all morning; is there anything you need me for?'

Colin was unsure whether or not he should discuss his assessment with Jason. On the one hand, it would help gauge the response of Helena and Mike, and it could potentially help forestall some of their concerns. Jason seemed to know both Helena and Mike pretty well. Colin was unsure, however, whether he wanted to bring Jason in on his proposal, considering he was going to be leaving the next day.

'Come in, please, come in', replied Colin, still uncertain how to proceed. 'I've been working on that presentation for Helena tomorrow.'

'How's it going?'

'I think I've a good draft done. I might read over it again later once I've had a break from it so I can try to look at it fresh again.'

'And what's the general gist?'

'Well, what would it be if you were to write it?'

'For a start I'd hire your role in New York where the IT management are based. I'd increase the testing capability to crank through the test cases more quickly and I'd get another business analyst or two to help with documenting all the change requests as they come through.'

'Do you think Helena and Mike would be expecting those recommendations?'

'Well, they are more or less the recommendations we came to at the last onsite here in Singapore – about the time you were being interviewed. Of course, Mike shot down the suggestion that your role be hired in New York, but other than that it's pretty consistent.'

For some reason Colin could not quite place, he decided against sharing his findings with Jason. He already knew, simply on the basis of Mike's disposition to having the PM, if not the whole team, in Singapore, that he would not be happy with much of the proposal. Neither did he need Jason to tell him – on the basis that Mike believed the budget was on track – that he would not be happy with Colin's conclusions about the budget. He was coming to realise that his conclusions were a sword that he would have to live by or die by.

'Okay, thanks for that, Jason. I'll do some more work on the presentation and feed some of that back into the conclusions.'

'If you like I can review it for you and give you a few pointers in terms of how Mike and Helena are likely to react to your perspective on our programme. It might help to soften the blow.'

Colin was not sure he liked how Jason referred to *his* perspective on *their* programme, as if somehow he was still an uninvolved outsider. Then again, maybe it tied in with his earlier thoughts that he was the auditor and the executioner.

'I think I'll just work on it a bit more for now – it's not ready for review yet – but thanks for the offer.'

'Okay', replied Jason, raising his hands in the air. 'If you need anything else just let me know', he continued and walked out of the door. Just before he closed it he turned back. 'One thing that I forgot to mention is that Mike is an absolute stickler for format. You should send the pack on to Daisy for formatting. She will put it in the right corporate format, colours, font and all of that.'

'I think I should be fine, thanks. The slides are more of a guide to the conversation than an end in themselves.'

'Look, Colin, trust me on this. It's your call, but I have seen meetings totally destroyed because Mike didn't get a table in the format he's used to. In the past he's simply declared things unreadable in their current format and postponed the meeting. Sometimes there have been other reasons for wanting to postpone and he's just used this as an excuse, but it gives him the option. Other times I've seen him spend ten minutes of a thirty-minute meeting picking at things he would have liked to see differently. Daisy is used to this and has done all of our presentations. She's pretty good. Anyway, as I said, it's your call.' With that Jason left.

While Colin did want the presentation to be kept to a close circle, he didn't want Mike to railroad the meeting over formatting concerns. He knew Mike had a pretty strong personality and could only imagine that as a peer Helena would have to listen thoughtfully to any of his concerns. He would have to send Mike and Helena the presentation in advance of the meeting and Mike would have plenty of reasons to postpone once he saw it. Against his own wish to keep the circle closed he decided he could not afford to take this risk. He thought, however, that he should brief Daisy before sending her the file.

'Daisy, do you have a minute, please?'

'Sure', Daisy replied, getting up and following Colin into his office. 'If it's about the stakeholder management spread-sheet, I haven't got to that yet – I've been really busy. Jason also asked that I triage the defects and change requests. I'm really not going to get to this until next week, just to manage your expectations.'

While he had only asked for this help the day before, Colin would have expected that Daisy would at least have started. He really had no idea what else she had on her plate, but it wasn't something he wanted to get into now.

'Okay, Daisy, I understand. I wasn't looking to speak to you with regard to the stakeholder management informa-tion, but it is of course important. What I wanted to do was to give you something else to do. I need this done by the end of the day today, it's not a big job, and it's only lunchtime now, so you should have enough time if you prioritise this over all of your other work.'

'Sure. What is it?' replied Daisy with obvious irritation.

'Well, it's actually quite delicate. I've put together my own view on the areas of the project that need to be reviewed to get things back on track. In a way I have presented an extreme view so the conversations can begin on how far in that direction we should go as a programme. At this stage these are only ideas, so I want to ensure that they go to Helena and Mike only so we can agree on the way forward before distributing them.'

'And what do you want from me?'

'I would like you to format the presentation with tables, graphs and text in the Bank IB standard format that Mike is used to seeing.'

'Sure, I can do that.'

'As I said, the content is a bit more extreme than you might expect and it hasn't been syndicated, so I'd appreciate it if this could be kept confidential.'

'I get it.'

'Also, of course, as you read it, if you have any concerns please just come and see me to talk about it.'

'Okay.'

'All right, then', replied Colin, feeling frustrated at Daisy's apathy, annoyance or outright distain. 'So I'll pass this on to you now and I'd appreciate it if you could return it, to me only, by the end of your day.'

'Right.'

'Okay, thanks', replied Colin. Daisy had already begun to walk away. 'One more thing, Daisy; you mentioned you're particularly busy at the moment. I really don't want the team burning out with the workload. Could you please send me an email outlining all the work you currently have on your plate once you get back to your desk so I can also manage what I send your way?'

'I'm going to lunch now. I'll get to it later', Daisy replied without turning round, and left the office.

Colin was pretty shocked at Daisy's attitude but decided that this was a challenge he would have to deal with the following week at the earliest. For now he needed her to do what he hoped was a pretty straightforward administrative task that was well within her capabilities, at least according to Jason, who was one person who might have actually seen any output from her in the past. He wondered if she, too, was about to hand in her notice. His gut told him that she had already bailed out, realising that working with him might just be a bit too hard. He attached the draft deck to an email and hit the 'send' button, regretting it even as his finger left the mouse. He didn't know why and didn't dwell on it because it was already too late. He decided to get something to eat.

As he headed for the lift he thought that he would begin to try to get to know some of his other operations colleagues not in the programme. It would be good to get other perspectives on operations, people, processes and culture. It would be also good to go to lunch with people working in similar situations, to bounce ideas and situations around and to get other opinions. There was the usual queue for the lift and it took at least five minutes just to get out of the building. He felt his phone vibrating in his pocket and he answered just as he stepped into the midday heat.

'What the hell do you think you're playing at?'

'Hello, who is this?'

'It's Serge! Who did you think it was?'

'Wow, Serge, it's pretty late there', replied Colin, more shocked that Serge was calling him at eleven at night in New York than at Serge's aggression. Serge was practically screaming, and he could hear music in the background.

'Look, Colin, enough of the niceties. What do you think you are doing with this project review?'

Though Colin was surprised at the delayed reaction from their conversation the night before, he felt positive that at least Serge was contacting him to talk about it instead of completely stonewalling him.

'I'm glad you called me about that. I was hoping you would have sent something through last night for inclusion in the analysis so we could present this as a joint review. I put together a draft deck today; I was hoping to speak to you later about it.'

'You have to be kidding me. You call this a joint review? If you had been looking to present a joint review it would have been balanced, but this is absolutely damning. Roberto was right!'

'I'm sorry, I don't follow you. What are you talking about?'

'Your so-called review! I have it in front of me. You damn the project as it's been run and you put me out of a job. How is that a joint review?'

Colin was gobsmacked. Daisy had sent the presentation to Serge, or she had sent it to Jason and he had sent it to Serge. Either way, she had completely ignored his request for confidentiality. He should have trusted his gut.

'I would have preferred to talk you through it, Serge, but it seems that someone thought it would be better if they sent it to you directly. I can talk about it now if you like, but it sounds like you're pretty wound up already ...'

'Wound up? Damn right I'm wound up. You're suggesting my role is moved out of New York. You're effectively firing me', screamed Serge, partly out of anger and partly to make himself heard above the music that seemed to get louder and fade at intervals as if someone was opening and closing a door to a bar or club.

'Then I'm firing myself too, Serge, as I've recommended my own role be located in Europe as well.'

'Look, if you have some burning desire to move to the land of pralines that's your problem but if you ... that ... just ... can ...'

'Serge, I can't hear you over the music. Can you go somewhere quieter if you want to talk about this now? But it would be probably best to continue the discussion when you're back at work', Colin replied, but found he was talking to a dead line.

Colin had been walking as he talked – because he had had to shout to be heard over the noise on the other end of the line he wanted to move as far away as possible from the Bank IB building. Only now did he realise that his shirt was wet and sticking to his body. He was livid. Jason and Daisy had stitched him up. He had expected a strong reaction but he had hoped to control it, at least to some degree. Now he needed to go into damage limitation mode. It would have to be a sandwich after all.

He started walking back to the office, shaking his head as he went, unsure whether he was more angry at Daisy for her total disrespect for his wishes or at himself for his own naivety. He marched past the sandwich counter, which had a queue arching around by the cooler shelves. He would have to give lunch a miss. Daisy and Jason were not at their desks when he walked back to his office. This at least was positive, as he did not want to confront them. First, he wanted to be calm, and second, it would not improve the situation in any way. Jason was off the project already and Daisy was also soon to be part of the project history book.

Colin needed to talk to Helena to at least give her a heads-up on what was going on, if not to try to contain the situation in some way. If Serge had the presentation, so did Roberto. It may have already got to Helena. He opened up his email and the first one he saw was from Daisy.

Colin,
This is formal notice of my resignation. My husband, Jason, has secured me alternative employment working in a regional team at his new place of work.

Regards,
Daisy Tan (Goh)

Colin's jaw nearly hit the floor. Jason Tan and Daisy Goh were married! Daisy had reported to Jason. He had had direct control of her pay, her bonus and her performance ratings. He did not even know where to start on how wrong he thought this was.

The next email was from Helena with no content, just a subject line: 'We need to talk. Please call me.'

Colin saw that Helena was online so he put on his PC headset and clicked the video link.

'Helena. Hi. Thanks for making yourself available so quickly.'

'Well, it was I who wanted to speak to you, Colin.'

'Yes, obviously. What I mean is you're taking the time to help contain the leak of my report before our meeting.'

'I'm sorry, Colin, but I have no idea what you're talking about. I'm calling you about Daisy Goh.'

'Tan.'

'What?'

'Tan. Her name is Tan, not Goh.'

'Colin, I'm not sure what you're going on about, but it's not a time to be pedantic.'

'I'm sorry, maybe we do need to step back. Did Daisy send her resignation letter to you as well?'

'HR informed me thirty minutes ago that Daisy resigned, citing her reasons as your inappropriate behaviour. She has stated to HR, for the record, that you have arrived to the office in wet see-through shirts, inappropriately revealing cycling attire, that you had insinuated on occasion, with some double entendre, that she thought you were "hot", and that while you involved the male staff in your assessment and planning, you gave her tasks that she termed little more than secretarial work.'

'You have got to be kidding.'

'Unfortunately, I'm not "kidding", as you put it.'

'Were you aware that Daisy Goh was a direct report of her husband, Jason Tan?'

'Not until this morning. Look, to be honest with you I wanted to bring it to your attention because HR rightly makes a point of investigating all claims. Even if all of the above were true it would be dealt with in the first instance with a warning. If you had made inappropriate comments about Daisy it might have been more serious, but that does not seem to be the case. Given the fact that Jason and Daisy didn't exactly stay on the right side of HR we think this is simply a shot over the bows to leave well enough alone and allow them both to leave in peace.'

'Fine, but the fact that a claim was made will remain on my record.'

'Yes, that's true, but it will also contain the results of the investigation. There is nothing we can do about this.'

'This is plain wrong.'

'That might be true, but my advice to you is to co-operate with HR, give full details of your response to the accusations, let HR come to the expected conclusion and move on.'

Helena adjusted her gaze slightly so that instead of looking at the video of him on her computer she was staring straight at the camera. Colin knew that she had spoken the last word on the matter. He could not undo the words Daisy had written to HR.

'I assume she's on gardening leave?'

'Yes. You won't see her or Jason again. Now tell me, what is this you wanted to say about your review? We have a meeting planned to discuss this, right?'

'I've just forwarded it to you now. Let me know when you have it opened. Daisy and Jason left me a parting gift. Jason convinced me that I should send it to Daisy to have it format-ted correctly and Daisy or Jason forwarded it to Serge. I had meant to discuss it with Serge tonight.'

'I'm looking through it now', interrupted Helena; Colin tried to read her facial expressions as she skimmed through the document.

'My conclusions are pretty drastic by Bank IB standards, it seems, and also include co-location of the team in Brussels. Serge called me and was pretty angry. I'm guessing Mike might also get to see it if Serge or Roberto forwards it to him. I'm not sure he will be ecstatic at the proposal either.'

'Colin, this is good. Not the mess-up in communication, I mean; the proposal itself. I need to look at it in more detail, but I can support the conclusions. Mike is going to hate it, but don't let that worry you. If the cat is out of the bag you won't get it back in. It was not forwarded to me as you thought it would be, so you have still time to regain control of the message.'

'You mean you think that Serge may not have forwarded it further?'

'I'm guessing he did, but New York is not in for another few hours so you have time to send it with an appropriate message to Roberto and Mike and also invite Roberto to the call tomorrow.'

'Shouldn't I bring the call forward?'

'No, there's no panic. As you know, I am in London this week for an operations executive onsite meeting and Mike is here too, so you don't need to worry about him storming into your office in the meantime. Try to avoid him if he tries to call. I think it would be best if we went through this one together. I would, however, recommend that you take Jason's advice even if you think it wasn't given in good faith. Mike is actually a stickler for format and it can be distracting once he gets going. Jason's reasons could even have been legitimate until he saw the content. I would recommend that Suria do this for you. He is pretty good at that sort of thing, will see this practically and is trustworthy. Then send it to Mike, Roberto and me explaining that it is a discussion draft.'

'Okay, I'll discuss this with him now, I can see that he's outside.'

'Fine, but do try and get it out before five today – any longer and you'll have missed the opportunity to bring this back at least a little bit into our control. I'll also talk to Christine Kale as no doubt she will be dragged into this before we know it. I'll talk to you later, Colin. Chin up, and strap yourself in for the ride.'

9

Dealing with Difficult Stakeholders

Colin hit the 'send' button at exactly six in the evening Singapore time – five in the morning in New York and eleven in the morning in Brussels. He had already begun to think of time in this way and looked forward to the clocks springing forward, first bringing New York an hour closer in mid-March and then Brussels and London by the end of the month.

Helena had been right on all counts. There had been no more noise on the review while New York slept, Suria took the information in the slides in the most pragmatic way and he was able to turn them into Bank IB standards in no time at all. Colin kicked himself once again just for good measure for not including Suria in the first place. Before leaving for home Colin updated the invitation to include Roberto. He then changed into his 'revealing' cycling attire and got on his bike.

Though the sun was low in the sky, casting an orange glow across the water, he had lost the sense of wellbeing that had filled him during his morning cycle. As if on cue, dark cumulus storm clouds built, billowed and rolled like a black toxic smoke. He could see the wall of rain ahead even as the sun still shone on the path where he was cycling. The sky exploded in an ear-splitting crack and as he neared where the wall of wet met the dry asphalt he stopped and looked in awe at the natural phenomenon. Feeling as though he were standing on the precipice behind a waterfall, he stood looking at the deluge no more than half a metre away. For an amazing full minute, which felt like forever, he felt only the cool air created by the movement of the water from the sky. Then the bouncing drops hit his feet and a moment later he was engulfed and wet through. He couldn't help but see it all metaphorically and, even drenched and fighting to see a few feet in front of him, he smiled to himself and allowed himself to enjoy the feeling of rain on his skin. Singaporeans were always dumbfounded when he mentioned his amazement at the Singapore rain, as if, coming from Ireland, he should be used to rain. In Ireland there were soft days, drizzle, heavy rain, showers and a hundred other types of rain, but nothing like this. It might rain in Ireland for a month solid but when measured by the amount of water falling, Ireland didn't come close to Singapore. He was fond of relating that while average rainfall in Ireland was about two millimetres per hour, Singapore could reach sixty times this amount and then some.

The road outside his house was dry. Either it hadn't rained there or it had already evaporated. Except for the fact that Colin was still drenched to the bone, it was as if it had never happened.

When he had showered, changed and put the children in bed he finally began to answer the question Clara had innocently put to him as he squelched in the door. She had simply asked how his day had been. He watched as with every detail her eyes opened wide with incredulity and her jaw dropped in disbelief.

'I thought they played politics at ACB, but this is a whole new level.'

'I'm hoping the worst is behind me.'

'I think that's just your optimism speaking. You have yet to deal with the infamous Mike Gretchen.'

'You could be right. I've got to talk to Serge this evening. With any luck he will have calmed down, but it's still unlikely to be a pleasant conversation.'

'With any luck he'll be sober, you mean.'

'I never said he was drunk.'

'Get real, Colin, you didn't have to. Eleven at night, loud music, voices coming and going? He was probably calling you from the toilets of his local bar.'

'You can speculate, but it makes no difference to me. He reacted then and it changed nothing.'

'Maybe. Just be careful. From what you've told me Helena sounds great, but you're relying on her support completely.'

Clara was right. It seemed that after just four days into the role battle lines had been firmly drawn and while he didn't fire the first shot, he had created the ammunition. It had been a crazy four days. He felt tired, it was eight o'clock and his first, and unusually his only, call was the one he had arranged himself with Serge at eleven, so he had three hours to spare. He looked across at Clara's wine glass, at the beads of condensation rolling down where the warm, humid night air hit the glass and was cooled by the wine. Even the glasses sweated in the Singapore night. He remembered sitting in a taxi, stuck in traffic, soon after he arrived. It was an old Toyota Crown that had probably done half a million kilometres around the island, like a rat in a cage. The air conditioning was blasting from the vents and the driver was wearing a jacket. He would have asked for the aircon to be turned down but for the relief it gave from the stench of pandanus leaves lying behind his headrest on the recess under the back window. The windows had fogged up and, remembering how he used to draw figures on the car window as a kid, he had drawn a sweeping circular line on the window with his finger, but the initial stroke of a master-piece smiley face failed to appear. The condensation was, of course, on the outside while he sat in the cold within. As he contemplated breaking his own rule and having a glass of wine, his phone rang.

'Hi, this is Colin speaking.'

'Hi, Colin, this is Serge.' Colin mouthed 'Serge' to Clara, who leant closer. 'Look, about my call last night, I was obviously pretty upset with the deck that was sent through, but …'

'The way it was communicated to you wasn't ideal. I think that exacerbated the situation', Colin interrupted, trying to spare Serge further anguish.

'Yeah, that's true, but it was late and I … I didn't say anything that, I mean, did I say anything that you …?'

'You told me that you were unhappy with the project appraisal, and that's fine. I know the co-location piece was a shock, and maybe you felt that the assessment was some-what harsh, but now you've had time to think it over, could you let me know any factual inaccuracies that you feel need to be corrected?'

'Its more the remediation I have concerns with. I mean, throwing out the vendor, moving the project team location, going back to basics. It all seems a bit drastic.'

'You could be right, Serge, but that's the subjective bit. That's the bit I personally recommend and I stand by it. It is, of course, up to those on a higher pay grade than me to make the ultimate decisions. I know you're not delighted with it, but could you tell me are there any of the problems as stated that you disagree with?'

There was silence, and Colin could not make out if Serge was just not ready to respond to the question at seven in the morning after what could have been a late night before or if he was truly indecisive about the answer.

'Truth is, though a lot of it makes sense it feels like I'm seeing it for the first time. You'll have to give me some time to respond.'

'That's fine, Serge. I had a meeting set up to talk to you later on this, let's go through it then.'

'Tell you what. Let's just give it a miss and I'll review it properly and respond by email. If you want to get me early tomorrow before your call with senior management I'll be available.'

After hanging up Colin reached across the table for the bottle of wine.

'You were way too easy on him. I would have hung him out to dry.'

'That's because you're a tough cookie and I'm just a big softie', Colin smiled as he began to pour himself a glass.

'Your rule didn't last long', said Clara with a smile.

'The rule is I don't drink when I'm working. Now I have no calls left for the night. Not a single one. I can just sit here and do nothing but chat with you. Maybe for a change even we can talk about something other than the project and the people working on it', said Colin, replacing the wine bottle on the table. As he did his phone rang again. Clara rolled her eyes.

'Colin, this is Helena. The call has been moved forward at Mike's insistence; apparently he's flying back to Singapore during the allotted time tomorrow. He's got Roberto as well and they've asked to discuss the deck in fifteen minutes. Are you free?'

At the end of the call Colin pushed his wine across the table to Clara whose glass was empty.

'It doesn't stop, does it?' Clara asked.

'Not tonight, at least', replied Colin.

He got up from the table and walked behind Clara, leaned down and put his arms around her, laying his cheek against hers.

'I love you, you know that, don't you?' he whispered in her ear.

'I know, but that won't make it easier if we only get to see each other on weekends.'

'I know.'

'Go. Let's not worry about it now. Get yourself ready and good luck. With the way the day has gone so far, you'll need it.'

Colin gave Clara a last squeeze and a kiss on the cheek and left her behind with his glass of wine. When he closed the door to his office area he immediately turned on the air conditioning. He had installed an ultra-quiet model so that he could work in the room in peace. He had five minutes to spare before the call, so he opened up the presentation pack and read through it again in preparation. He was nervous. Though it felt as though he had been working on the project for months, his assessment came after just four days in the role. Was it too early? Should he have requested more time? Either way, it was all too late now. Reading through the presentation, it still made sense to him and he was ready to stand by his conclusions. He put on his headset and clicked the link on the invitation sent by Helena. He could see on the list of participants that automatically appeared that he was still the only person on the phone. There was a beep and the list showed that a guest had joined.

'Hello, this is Colin on the line. Who else has joined?'

There was no reply for a moment and then there was another beep.

'Hello', said Colin again. 'This is Colin, who else is on the line?'

'Hi, Colin, this is Helena and I'm in the conference room here in London with Mike and Roberto.'

'Hi, everyone. I think someone else may have joined too', said Colin, who was also surprised that Roberto was in London. He wondered if he had got the presentation from Serge earlier in the day before he had sent the revised version.

'Let's just get started', replied Helena. 'We really don't have time to worry about the technical anomalies.'

'Okay', replied Colin, slightly put out by Helena's tone. 'Thank you all for taking the time today. As you know, I started only this week in the role as project manager for the collateral project which will functionalise the collateral process, align roles and responsibilities to emerging regulations, reduce booking and processing risk, and increase automation.'

'Yes', interrupted Mike, 'you're right. You were hired to project manage it and not to tear it apart.'

Collin paused. He didn't know whether he was expected to answer that or if Helena would somehow show some support. There was continued silence on the other end. Colin wondered for a moment if they were on mute, but he could see by the participant list on his screen that the line was active, open and unmuted.

'Mike, Roberto, Helena, I'm happy to present this in any way you think it is best. I can take you straight through the presentation and we can discuss at the end, or we can discuss the slides one by one. It's up to you.'

'Just continue, please, Colin', Helena replied.

'Okay', continued Colin. 'We don't need to spend time on the first slide; it simply gives the context behind some of the changes in direction that the project has taken, which in turn have contributed to some of the issues we are currently dealing with, which we'll get to as we go through the presentation.'

'We don't need a history lesson', Mike interjected.

'Then let's move on to the main discussion. The next part of the discussion moves on to the areas in the project that I have observed to be contributing to the delay in the schedule and overrun in the budget.'

'So you say', interjected Mike again.

'That's correct, Mike', replied Colin, beginning to lose patience but still maintaining a calm, level tone. 'These are things that I say. On the one hand, during the presentation I will be presenting facts that I hope can go undisputed as they are in no way dressed up. I will then be presenting my view on facts that I believe are causing project issues and my personal recommendation for remediation. Again, if you would prefer to proceed in another way please let me know.'

'Oh no', replied Mike, 'by all means continue. There is nothing like the sound of a man digging his own grave.'

Colin chose to ignore the last remark. 'The first area that has been problematic for the project is the dispersion of key project staff.'

'It's a global project, for God's sake, what do you expect? It impacts each of the regions in different ways, so it makes sense to run it this way.'

'While it might make sense to have representation in each region to ensure that all requirements are taken into account, running the project from Singapore adds no advantage when the region is no more impacted than any other region, especially when the IT management are based in New York.'

'The head of the global function sits in Singapore so it makes most sense for the project to be run here.'

'Mike, as global function owner and the project sponsor, you have the right to decide. It's my responsibility, however, to make you aware that this dispersion is detrimental to the success of the project and I have listed specific reasons and impacts on this slide.'

'The reasons are bull! You guys need some toughening up. It seems to me like too many people are afraid of a little hard work. Sounds to me that someone might be angling for a sweet international assignment in the land of moules-frites with a Smurfette to keep him company.'

'The next area', continued Colin, 'relates to the core documentation of the programme, or more precisely the lack of usable quality documentation. This is causing us issues on a daily basis.'

'Again, the project management speak. TOMs and BRDs and FRDs and the like. If you guys had your way you would be happy to create a mountain of paper and nothing else.'

'Mike, I would be happy for you to join any one of our testing calls so you can experience first hand the impact of not having proper documentation in place and how inexperienced and unqualified the vendor resources are. Besides experiencing how painful it is trying to drive out requirements during a project testing phase, you will also come to realise very quickly what a waste of time, effort and money it is to run a project in this way.'

'Oh, we're on to budget are we? I was looking forward to that discussion. So we've spent less money than forecast, but by some miracle of project management calculations we have overspent. Is that right?'

'I was going to cover budget a little later in the deck, but if you would prefer to cover this first I'm happy to do so. You stated absolutely correctly that we have spent less money this year than forecast. The project also spent less money last year than was forecast. The problem is that the deliveries that were associated with the budget spend were not all made. If the project continues in this way we could spend less than the allocated budget every year until the forecast total budget has run out and we will have delivered nothing tangible.' Colin paused, waiting for Mike to interject, but he said nothing. 'The formulae and ratios state how bad things are. The schedule performance index is simply calculated by putting the budget of the work done over the budget of the work that was supposed to have been done during that time. A ratio of one means that we did what we said we would do when we said we would do it. Anything less is not so good.

The ratio is forty-six per cent. In other words, we have only done half of what we said we would do in the allotted time. The problem is that we spent well over forty-six per cent of the budget allotted to those tasks; that's the next index shown here, the cost performance index. This is at sixty-two per cent, which basically means that for every dollar we spent we got sixty-two cents of value from it.'

'This has to be wrong', interrupted Mike finally. 'If this is all true and we have delivered less of the work than scheduled and we have paid more than expected for the work that has been done, how can we still be showing that we are twenty-five per cent under budget last year?'

'Again, Mike, it's exactly because we're behind schedule. If we did all of the things we were supposed to and engaged different teams earlier and if we were exactly on time, while getting only sixty-two cents on the dollar benefit for every dollar spent we would be significantly over budget. Said mathematically, if you multiply our schedule performance index by the inverse of our cost performance index the answer is exactly the seventy-five per cent of the budget allocated that you mentioned.'

Colin was really feeling the disadvantage of presenting over the phone. If he had been sitting in the same place as the others he would have attempted to read the room. He didn't know whether Roberto was sitting there shaking his head or if Helena was nodding agreement. He heard nothing from either of them; instead he had Mike poking holes in his analysis at every turn. While he felt that his message was getting through, he was conscious that he was making no friends. It was then that he was first struck by the fact that he had not questioned the choice of sponsor. Not specifically whether Mike should be a sponsor, but why there was no other sponsor. In the past the operations team would have done most of the work. Perhaps initially the original sponsor had planned to take everything including booking and pricing and no one ever thought to realign the sponsorship with the new purpose of the project. He kicked himself now that he had not thought of this either.

'Colin, are you still on the line?' asked Helena.

'Yes, yes, I'm here', replied Colin.

'Could you answer the question then, please?'

Colin realised that he must have tuned out for a minute as he thought about the situation and the sponsorship question. He suddenly realised how tired he was. It was just his fourth night into the role and he already felt physically and mentally exhausted.

'I'm sorry, the connection seemed to have dropped for a second, could you repeat, please?

'Maybe you'd be better off working in the office instead of taking calls from the comfort of your home. I asked where the money is going', said Mike.

Tempted as he was to respond to the first comment, Colin ignored what he had begun to view as highly unprofessional conduct. This could not be anyone playing a part, or thinking strategically; it seemed to be completely irrational behaviour. It was then he realised that Mike was on the ropes. Whether it was Colin's intention or not, every slide, every word was a body blow and Mike was flailing his arms in any way he could.

'Unfortunately, Mike, the money is going directly to Indo-Sign. Currently, under the contract as it is written, they are incentivised to deliver bad code. Every day fixing issues extends the testing period. They have been paid by the day since the scheduled end of the systems integration testing. The longer it goes on, the more we pay them. On top of that, they command an extra development fee for everything they term a change request. As we have little documentation to back up our position, this is very easy for them to do.'

Colin held back from emphasising this with the statistics of defects found and the failure rate of fixes implemented.

He hoped he would not have to reiterate them. They were in the presentation; that was enough.

'So your recommendation is to completely release the team that has built up institution and project experience. If we were to take your half-baked ideas seriously, don't you think we'd be shooting ourselves in the foot to lose the development team that knows what we're doing inside out?'

'That is one view, Mike, and I would be happy specifically on this one to take your lead and the lead of the IT team who own the relationship, but personally, I would prefer not to work with a vendor that has been disingenuous and that has taken advantage of a bad situation. If it had just been the fact that the contract was bad, that could be corrected with a renegotiation, but, as the statistics show, their defect rate is double the industry average, their defect turnaround time is three times what has been experienced on other projects and their failure rate of delivered fixes is incredibly bad', said Colin, inwardly wincing and wondering if he could have avoided twisting the knife.

'And then you want to practically double the staff when you've already said that the project is running over budget?'

'It's my firm belief that this will actually reduce the spend on the project if managed properly. Today we are paying the vendor to lead us up the garden path and we're taking the project team, IT, business and subject matter experts from the line with us. We're wasting our time. This way we set a solid foundation and begin to move on.'

'I can't believe this. I was convinced to bring you on. I was told that you knew what you were doing and had turned projects around before. What you want to do here is start it again. It's complete bull and you are as incompetent as the rest of them.'

Colin bit his tongue. There was a reason Roberto and Helena were silent, and it was not because they were in agreement.

Colin tried to bring Mike around using the language Mike himself had used on Colin's second day into the job.

'You gave me an analogy once that you were the general waging the war and I was leading the charge in this battle. Well, I've been to the front and I can report that it's a mess down there. It's littered with bodies and the troops are fighting as long and hard as they can against a sophisticated, well-equipped enemy. They themselves are armed with nothing more than paper swords and there are storm clouds on the horizon. I'm asking to return to the front with a message from you that we should pull back, regroup, and gather new armaments. Once we have completed the groundwork and won this battle we will then have a fighting chance to win the war.'

'God, that was brilliant', Mike replied sarcastically. 'Can someone give me a bucket? I'm about to throw up. That's got to be the cheesiest thing I have heard in all of my career.'

Colin was now just too tired and too angry to care any more. His vision seemed to shake for a second and he felt heat in his face that the air conditioning did nothing to alleviate. He took a deep breath and tried to remain calm and focused. He continued now, as he felt he had to continue: 'One of the things that I didn't include in the pack, because I hoped to discuss it with you in person, Mike, is the sponsorship of the programme.'

'What about it?' replied Mike.

'I think we should also consider a shared sponsorship responsibility with the front office, considering the shared responsibility in the final target state process.'

'You like war analogies, Conor? Well, this is insubordination, it's treason. This is none of your damn business, and punishment for treason is a shot to the head. Do you understand me?'

'Mike, I've heard about enough, thank you', replied a voice that Colin did not immediately recognise and noticed that it came from the guest speaker who had not been announced. 'I think it's best that we end this call now and regroup when appropriate to discuss next steps.'

The line in London hung up, followed by the extra guest line. Colin finally hung up. It was then he realised. The other voice was Christine Kale.

10

International Relocation

Colin was happy to close the door of the Mercedes behind him and feel the warmth blow from the vents. It was already late March and the winter hung back obstinately, preferring to linger in the developed architecture of the northern hemisphere where it could be most effective. He'd breathed deeply on leaving the terminal, taking in the cool air, refreshing and welcome but for the infusion of cigarette smoke from the waiting passengers and the emissions of the taxis running their engines to keep their cabins warm.

'Rue au Beurre, please', said Clara, leaning forward from where she was jammed between the children's car seats in the back.

The taxi pulled out and the meter began to tick forward faster than the clock. The voices from behind with their curious questions and patient answers began to merge into a background soundtrack with the radio. Colin breathed on the window and drew a smiley face.

'Please don't do that', ordered the taxi driver in a voice as strong in tone as it was in accent, leaving no doubt that it was to be obeyed and bringing Colin back momentarily to full awareness of his surroundings.

The driver hit a button on the meter that added another ten euros to the rate. Colin wondered for a moment if it was to pay to have the windows cleaned following his artistic endeavours, feeling that common sense of unease brought about by a lack of common understanding of the norms.

'Airport charge', stated the driver gruffly, aware of Colin's gaze.

Colin didn't feel like arguing; he just wanted to get his family to the serviced apartment. He had no idea of the standard charges, they were not on the inside of the window as they were in Singapore, and Bank Investissement Belgique would be paying for this ride anyway. While he hated the feeling of being ripped off, he turned back towards the window and did not reply.

It was the last Friday in March and seven weeks to the day since Helena had called him to let him know that the recommendations he had made the night before would be taken to the executive board and would be carried. She had already secured support from Christina Kale as well as Marcel Janssens, who would shortly be named global head of collateral. He would also take on the role of operations sponsor for the programme, jointly with an as yet unnamed front office executive. Helena had said all of this in such a way that it sounded completely detached from the drama of the night before and had never even mentioned Mike Gretchen by name.

'Fortunately we will be able to bring forward some of the timelines you proposed in your presentation', she had continued. 'Roberto has been undertaking vendor assessments for some weeks now and is currently in final selection. The front-runner is Beldor, a Belgian specialist collateral consultancy firm, who will also be supported by PolDev, a software developer based in Wrocław in Poland.'

Even seven weeks later Colin was still in awe that in his first week on the job all of this had been going on around him without a breath of it even whispered. He still did not know whether he had been shepherded towards the conclusions he had made that seemed to fit so nicely with the plans already in motion, whether he had been hired with the knowledge that he would come to those conclusions or whether it was just chance – or fate, as Clara would have him believe; a foregone conclusion that all of the paths had been already drawn and we just had to walk forwards to meet at the predefined junction. Maybe it would not have mattered if he had come to completely different conclusions; maybe it was just more convenient that way.

'Morning rush hour', grunted the taxi driver as if surprised, swearing and feigning frustration as he slid into the gridlock. He raised his eyebrows, somehow believing that expressing surprise at the rush hour traffic, on the main route to the centre of Brussels, at seven thirty in the morning, was just the thing to absolve him of the expectation that it might be part of his job to know such things.

Colin stared back out the windows and looked at the unfamiliar number plates, noticing for the first time the relative quiet. He turned to see his family asleep in the back, Clara's head thrown back and turned sideways in a way that could prove painful when she awoke.

As if all it took was for Helena to say it for it to become so, Beldor had consultants on the ground two weeks later. They stuck to the numbers Colin had suggested. Six focused on initiating the target operating model, spending time in Singapore, Brussels, New York and London. Though they listened to the business representatives, they brought their own industry knowledge, which often trumped descriptions of some of the group's sacred cows. Within two weeks, two of the original six started on the requirements documentation and another two consultants were added to the team, leaving four each working on the target operating model and the requirements documentation. They were surprisingly efficient. While Colin would have liked to think that it was due to his direction and focus, he knew that much of it had to do with the fact that Mike was gone, and the belief was that he was gone because he did not get behind the project. There was now no incentive to even second-guess what was being done. Colin didn't see this necessarily as a good thing. Either way, a week before Colin left for Brussels, just four weeks after Beldor had arrived, they had secured sign-off of the future state roles and responsibilities for each of the major processes. This was no mean feat considering the level of process change between the front office and the operations group. In the new model no risk decisions could be made by operations and the front office was now responsible in all cases for selecting the correct type of collateral. Irrespective of any system deliverables, this was in itself a step change and one that could not have been achieved without the unwavering support of the new front office sponsorship, Jon Schrewed. The first draft of all end state process flows in the target operating model were also due by Monday, along with the business requirements first drafts. It felt like things were coming together.

Around the same time as the Beldor consultants started, PolDev led the code review overseen by Beldor and the results were due to be presented on Monday morning, fortuitously coinciding with his own permanent move to the Belgian office. Colin did not even know what to hope for. A review scathing of IndoSign coding, while validating his concerns, would mean additional time required for development and his estimated plan would need significant rework. A review that presented IndoSign in another light would cast doubt on his own review and the validity of the imposed rework. He tried to tell himself that it made no difference and each outcome would simply be a different starting point on the journey to the same place with different, equally eventful, ways of getting there. As the meter continued to remind him of the digits in the DeLorean moving back to the future, he thought that a bad code review would be tantamount to the taxi driver easing into the gridlock and throwing his hands in the air, while a good code review would be like taking the taxi on an off-road shortcut.

'It is now moving again', stated the driver humourlessly. Colin thought that it had never stopped.

'Where are we?' asked Clara, having been woken by the sudden outburst, slowly bending her head forward to a position that looked marginally less like the undead.

'No idea', replied Colin. 'Rest some more if you can, we're going nowhere fast.'

Clara seemed to take it in her stride. One of the advantages of fatalism is that believing the future has already been decided means that our only decision is how to enjoy it. But this was not something that Colin could enjoy, sitting in traffic in this taxi watching the meter rise with his own annoyance, even though it would not cost him a single cent. Helena seemed to be cut from a similar cloth as Clara, unmoved by circumstance while events happened around her, like polar equals kept apart by an invisible force. Here he was, propelled to the other side of the world, where he knew he would end up before a word was said. And when a word was said it was if proposals had been discussed ad nauseam before reaching the inevitable conclusion.

'I've asked Vikki Chong to put something in your calendar today', Helena had said. 'You will, I'm sure, want to discuss the terms of your move with your family before they are finalised. It will be good for you to have the details so you do not have to talk about it in the abstract.'

The funny thing was that Colin was not even surprised.

'That sounds reasonable', he said, even though presenting him with a one-way ticket out of the country in which he had spent a good portion of his adult life, a week into a new job, did not seem that reasonable at all. Yet here he was.

Vikki Chong was well prepared and Colin had to imagine that the relocation package had come from a standard menu where different options would be selected depending on the seniority of the mover, the current performance of the bank, and probably the mood of the requesting manager. It contained a lot of what he had heard would be standard; movement of household effects between current location and destination and temporary accommodation on arrival, for example. He lamented that the days of fully paid expatriation, including housing and private schools, seemed to have fallen by the wayside – along with the Lehman balance sheet – but he felt that all in all it was fair.

Looking back out of the window he could see the Botanic Garden on his right, so he knew from his research that they were not far from where they were going. A cyclist whizzed past in between the car and the gardens with his head down and backside in the air for a moment, leaving a blur of luminous pink in his wake.

'You should report him to HR', came a voice from the back and Colin turned to see Clara smiling at him as she watched him through half-open eyes. She held her body still as she spoke so as not to wake the children, who were leaning against her in various awkward poses.

'Do you think we were right to come here?'

'You know me Colin, I believe that we came here for a reason. Whether we think it is right or wrong is immaterial. Fate has brought us here and if we can remain open to all possibilities we might even understand why.'

'And you know me and therefore what I think of all that.'

'Sure, *you* think that *you're* here because *you* have control of *your* destiny and *you* decided to come here, so here *we* are.'

Colin snorted through his nose and grunted, 'I'm not so sure any more.'

'Well, that's a start', replied Clara, closing her eyes.

Colin turned back to the window and, looking across the trees in the Botanic Garden, thought of the coconut trees on the east coast of Singapore and what other differences Belgium would have in store. He had already been impressed with the Belgian team members who had come on board in the last few weeks. Some changes were introduced to the internal team too. Stefan Jacobs replaced Serge Baranov, who had been promoted to Roberto Giovanni's old role of head of collateral IT, BAU and projects. Roberto had moved at the same time to a front office IT role but was still involved in the project overseeing the front office IT delivery. Stefan's move was also through internal mobility and he had come from the securities IT team. Serge couldn't have been happier with the outcome and was surprisingly magnanimous in his further dealings with Colin. Stefan was an outspoken, by-the-book kind of guy from the start. On his first day he had stated, as if expecting strong push back, that he would need an end-to-end testing lead with experience in IT and business test management. As he said it, Colin realised it was something that he had not argued for in his presentation but that made eminent sense.

'I don't see a problem with test management getting funded', Colin had replied, but to no avail as Stefan continued to argue for it for another five minutes or so.

'You might feel that it is overkill', he continued, 'to have a full-time resource assigned full time, one hundred per cent, to this task, but let me assure you that the money spent up front in assigning someone to manage the testing efficiently will save five times the cost in the long run.'

'Yes, I agree. I have seen this in practice', Colin assured him.

'No, there is no question that it is required, even regression testing alone can be cut in half with proper coordination and automation. The test environment coordination alone can save countless hours of users' testing time. Ensuring that the test cases are written effectively and used and reused across all phases of testing can only mean shorter test cycles, in turn saving cost.'

'Stefan!' Colin almost shouted, 'I agree! And I'll ask Helena, Jon, Marcel and Serge to agree at the STC later today.'

'Okay, but just so that we are clear', and he was off again.

Colin hoped that working with Stefan face to face would be easier. He was incredibly detailed and very structured – very positive attributes in an IT delivery manager – but his intensity could be overbearing at times. While Colin would not want him to loosen up in his attitude to delivery, his communication approach could have been easier to deal with.

The test lead he did hire was just the type of person needed. Like many managers, Stefan's hiring technique, right or wrong, had revolved around looking for a clone of himself, and the person he found was just as detailed and structured but had somehow managed to slip by with some rounding of Stefan's weaknesses. Mija started soon after Stefan and since then she had shared various drafts of her test plans with Colin. She was also trilingual, speaking French and English as well as her native Polish. She was convinced that a programme of this size required its own testing group. Without support or prompting she drew up a business case for moving three New York-based IT business analysts off the project and using the same funds to secure an eight-person in-house testing team in Wrocław, where PolDev was based. The new team was assigned to write structured test cases with step-by-step instructions that could be used for unit testing, SIT and UAT, and that could be used at a later stage to create automated regression testing scripts.

'You are here', said the taxi driver triumphantly.

Colin was startled. His eyes were open and he had been staring out of the window but he had not even noticed that the car had stopped.

'How much do I owe you?'

'Like it says', replied the driver pointing at the meter, leaving Colin to wonder if he was afraid to say the number or if he did not trust his English.

'Seventy euros?' Colin said incredulously.

'Like it says', replied the driver.

Colin handed over newly minted notes and got out of the car to open the doors for his family to get out on the kerb side. The driver got out, lit a cigarette and opened the boot. Colin began to pull the bags one by one out of the boot and bring them over to the wall of the building. On his way back he glanced at the driver.

'Bad back', the driver said, smiling.

When he had unloaded and the taxi had driven off, Colin looked at his family standing with their bags outside the apartment building. They looked as if they had crossed the globe. Then he closed his eyes and grimaced as if in pain.

'What's wrong?' asked Clara.

'I forgot to get the receipt.'

11

Bigger Picture Project Management

It was one o'clock when the team gathered in the large conference room in the client enclave of the Bank IB building. The table was solid and imposing, the artwork on the walls whimsical and contemporary. There was a photograph of an old gas hob with stains of spilled coffee and a close-up of lichen growing on a wall and a rusted gate.

'You may not have got the email on Friday as you were in transit', Jörg said, 'but we completed the target operating model and business requirements drafts ahead of time on Thursday and so far we have had good feedback.'

Jörg was the lead consultant at Beldor and their single point of contact for all business and IT deliveries. He was pretty much clued in to everything that was going on but he wasn't shy about calling in any of his team if more detailed information was required.

'Let's not get too excited', interjected Marcel Janssens, 'we really have not had the chance to review the documents properly, but it is fair to say that so far we have been pleased with the level of detail and presentation of the materials. It has to be said that my operations teams collaborated pretty closely on these documents.'

'As did the front office team', Jon Schrewed opined, while the two sponsors jumping to take ownership of the outcome surprised Colin. If this continued the documents would be signed off in no time.

'It sounds to me like the dates for sign-off can be brought forward', suggested Helena.

'Unfortunately not', replied Jörg. 'I would say that we are on time and we will hit the dates we agreed as long as the operations and the front office can prioritise the review. We have people at the ready to incorporate the feedback into the work done to date. We do not want rushed acceptance. We have, however, accelerated the development of the functional requirements documents on the basis that we feel we have solid business requirements drafts to work on.'

'I haven't been close to the functional requirements documentation process', continued Helena. 'Who is writing these?'

'Our PolDev partners are writing them', answered Jörg.

'Isn't this part of the problem we had first time around?' asked Jon. 'We were provided functional specs from the vendor and they then coded on these and we found there were gaps between the requirements that we wanted and what they were contracted to develop.'

'The difference in this scenario', Colin said, speaking for the first time, 'is that Beldor are contracted against the business requirements, and irrespective of the "how" of the functional requirements document, the business requirements need to be met.'

'Does the business requirements process then also require an acceptance process from the vendor?' Helena asked.

'Yes', replied Jörg, 'another reason why we cannot rush the remaining sign-off period.'

'Jörg, I'm glad to see that the documentation is on track. What about the code?'

'The answer to the code quality is not as straightforward', began Jörg. 'The development is certainly off spec, and riddled with inconsistencies that, were they to have continued in development, would prove very difficult to manage in any testing phase. The database software and versioning is also incompatible with the coding compilers and will need to be replaced. On a more positive note, though coding modules are functionally incongruous, it maintains stylistic homogeneity and integrity throughout.'

'I have no idea what you just said', replied Marcel, looking over his glasses with raised eyebrows and furrows in his temple deep enough to plant potatoes.

'He means', began Helena, just managing to begin before Jörg made another attempt, 'that the foundation of the house is solid, but the kitchen has no sink and the bedroom has a cooker where the bed should be. The plumbing also needs to be replaced. Does the analogy suit, Jörg?'

'I think it's about right', replied Jörg.

'So what does that mean in terms of delivery?' asked Marcel, still evidently feeling that nobody was getting to the point.

'It means that broadly we believe that the situation can be rectified within the timeframes we initially agreed.'

'It sounds like IndoSign didn't do a bad job after all, then, if it takes so little time to fix', Jon contributed.

'Jon, from a technical perspective, we can manage the remediation', came the voice of Serge over the starfish conference phone, 'but from a business perspective, if it had continued, you would have had to cook your food in the bedroom, sleep in the bath and go to the neighbours for a glass of water.'

The room broke out into good-humoured laughter and while Serge was enjoying his moment of comedy Colin was pretty pleased that IT were firmly behind the decisions that had been made. Colin could not have asked for a better outcome from a credibility perspective. The evidence was there that the code had been going in the wrong direction, validating his push for remediation, but the effort required to bring it back on track allowed him to continue to hit his dates. He glanced across at his new front office sponsor, who for some reason was not amused, and was looking around at the laughing faces as if he felt they were laughing at him.

'Why are we doing this in the first place?' he asked.

'What do you mean, Jon?' asked Helena in a voice that seemed to say she cared about what he had to say and wanted to understand more. She could see that he was not one to lose face and regaining it could be painful.

'I mean, why are we doing this at all? I was briefed just this morning on the proposed Dodd–Frank rules, EMIR, their European cousin, and the cross-regulatory recommendations of BCBS–IOSCO. These new regulations will be coming into force within two years. By then it is likely to cost the bank too much to trade over-the-counter derivatives. Everything is going to be cleared by large clearing houses and the bilateral trading that this project is covering will largely disappear.'

'Now I am afraid I have no idea what you mean, Jon', came Serge's voice from the conference phone.

'I mean, Serge, that this is a dying business. By the time this is implemented there will be no more bilateral OTC derivative trades. There is no point in spending this money in the first place. Has nobody taken a step back and reassessed this in light of how the industry is moving? Has no one taken the time to smell the coffee?'

Colin had gone pale. He opened his mouth to say something that would surely make everything okay again but instead closed it again slowly. The voices continued and Jon ranted, excitedly but factually and logically. For a moment his voice faded into the background and Colin thought of John Newton. What was it he had said? 'When someone comes along and puts a stop to the progress we are making in achieving this goal we can, and do, feel personal loss as the goal to which we were committed will no longer be achieved.'

Colin felt it, and it was as if he could see it slipping away. He had just arrived in a foreign country to run a project he could see was being turned around and it was all collapsing with every word Jon spoke.

'Look, the regulations are being put in place', Jon went on, 'to safeguard the industry post the collapse of Lehman. OTC derivatives are viewed as the devil's instruments. All of this legislation is being put in place to eventually stop them being traded.'

'You're right', Helena said calmly. 'It is certainly the right time to reassess the business case in light of the Dodd–Frank regulations and other regulations that are coming into force.'

Helena paused, all eyes on her, and looked at Jon, who had an almost imperceptible smile as if satisfied that he had climbed back up to where he belonged. Helena continued carefully, wanting to support Jon on his pedestal while she spoke.

'We are probably lucky that we have ensured that the foundation code is reusable across many products. Jörg, does your analysis validate this?' she asked, pausing while Jörg merely nodded. 'Right, so that's positive. Jon, do we know how long it will take for OTCs to die completely or is it possible that there will be a long tail we will have to deal with for some time to come?'

'The industry is still in the analysis phase, but the writing is on the wall.'

'My understanding is that the legacy system is end of life so if we do not finish this project, which seems to be gaining momentum, we would need to initiate an upgrade of the legacy system to handle the remaining OTC volume. Is this an analysis you would recommend, Jon?'

Jon hesitated. He could see where this was going and he knew Helena well enough to know he was being given enough rope to tie up some conclusions, or to wrap around his neck. He also began to realise that whether or not the industry would move away from OTCs, they were going to be around for a long time to come and his business depended on the correct collateral processing that was required to trade them. There was also the issue of the trades that had been booked already that had long-dated expiry. It would be pretty difficult to suddenly make these disappear.

'As I said, the industry is clearly moving away from OTCs, and it is a good time to validate the business case. The fact that the hardware is end of life and we know that we need to support the business for some time to come, however, validates our need to build the foundation and deliver the OTC component before our legacy systems fall over.'

Colin, who had unconsciously been holding his breath, finally breathed again. Like it or not, he was pretty much tied to the project for a while and his fate would continue to be tied with its success. He couldn't even navigate the Belgian public transport system; what hope would he have navigating the job market without even a word of French or Flemish?

'I'll work on revalidating the business case with this new information and the estimates provided by Beldor to present at the next steering group', he said. 'At that point we should have all documentation completed and be a couple of weeks away from having the code ready to test in systems integration testing.'

'Thanks, Colin', Helena said, as if staking a claim on the moment's silence. 'I think in the last seven or so weeks we have taken the project out of a downward spiral and have begun to take control once again of the delivery. Besides the revised business case I would like to understand at the next STC further details on the test plans for systems integration testing, user acceptance testing and go-live cutover. Any other business?'

Nobody moved.

'Then let's reconvene in four weeks. I make that April the twenty-sixth.'

And with that everyone got up to leave and someone hung up the conference phone. Colin got up and slowly started packing his things away, as the other participants left. When they had gone he sat back in his chair and stared at the photo of the rusted gate, which was illuminated from behind. He thought he got the point; it was a gate, but as it had rusted solid to its hinges and had a gaping hole in the centre it was a gate no longer. It was useless, yet simply taking a picture of it and calling it art made it useful again. It felt to him that it was all about perception.

'Is everything all right, Colin?'

Helena was standing in the doorway. Colin wondered how long she had been there while he sat thinking about the use of rusty gates.

'Yes, thanks, fine. Just taking a moment to absorb the meeting and jot down a few points for the minutes while they're still fresh in my mind.'

'Jon is a strong supporter, but he is pretty new to project work. Sometimes I think we need a training course as rigorous for project sponsors as we have for project managers.'

'What's your view on the industry moves?'

'They don't matter for us right now. The delivery of this project, assuming we can keep to the timelines discussed, solves an immediate problem that will not go away any time soon. I do believe that the industry is changing – it needs to – but those changes are not even drafted yet, not to mind understood.'

'Fair enough, I'll get back to it so', he said, this time really gathering his things.

'He's been looking at it for the last ten years; it's only natural we should be drawn to take a moment ourselves.'

'I don't understand.'

'The gate', she said, and smiled for the first time. 'It is number one hundred. He's taken a hundred and twenty photographs of it, one a month for ten years. The red paint is shiny on number one. Some say it's about the passage of time, cycles and seasons, life and death. Others say that it's about our inevitable deterioration, fading into obscurity and still somehow having the ability to find beauty in that. I believe it's about the photographer himself, about dedication, hard work and discipline. Ten years of going to the same spot, in the same field, on the first day of every month, at midday, in the heat, the cold, the snow, slush and rain, through sickness, commitments, personal inconvenience and a variety of states of mind, knowing from the first day through to the one hundred and nineteenth that missing one day in twelve years would ruin what he had set out to achieve. Personally I find beauty in that. Enjoy your day.'

12

Test Planning

When Colin got back to his desk Mija was waiting for him. His smart card was not working yet so he could not plug his new laptop into the network or access the phone, as it was all run off the same security device.

'Hi, Colin, you said this morning that you'd have time to go over the test plans with me this afternoon. Is now convenient?'

'As convenient as any other time, I suppose, seeing that face to face is the only communication method that's working for me today.'

'Great, then let's go to the project area; I've printed the plan in large format and put it on the wall.'

The floor was part of the bank's new smart working environment. There were no fixed desks and no offices. Everyone had a locker and a laptop and could sit where they wanted within a designated area. There was a green garden area with plenty of plants, a yellow quiet area with no phones, grey areas with standard desks complete with large screens, and a large project area with interactive whiteboards, walls for printed project plans and a large central table. It was all pretty modern and bright and more what might be expected of an internet technology company's offices than a Belgian bank. There were, of course, financial reasons behind it as well as the general wellbeing of the workforce. Smart working meant at least twenty per cent less space was needed, as it was rare that more than eighty per cent of staff would be in the office at any one time, due to holidays, sickness, training, meetings or home working. All in all the bank and employees got quite a good deal. Of course it was a somewhat new experience for those who had enjoyed having their own office for a long time, but, as one would expect of pyramid-style management, they were in the minority.

'If you look here', said Mija, pointing to a visual representation of the plan on the wall, 'unit testing of the code has already begun for some of the modules where rewrite was not needed. This is iterative through the coding cycle as specific units or small modules are complete. It will finish then at the same time as the coding cycle ends. The coding is actually scheduled to complete a week before it is shown on the plan, but a week of extra unit testing is built in.'

Mija was pointing at a Gantt-style chart with long horizontal bars cutting across time representing the phases of the project. Where one phase was dependent on the next an arrow joined the end of one bar at a point in time to the start of another. In some cases the Gantt chart dependency line went straight to the bar below it, for example at the end of the bar representing systems integration testing an arrow went one line below to the start of user acceptance testing. In some cases there were multiple dependency lines that cut across various activities. User acceptance testing had a dependency on completing the test cases as well as test environment availability. As project manager Colin owned the master soft copy of the plan, but in some cases work package owners had broken out their own sections into further detail with subtasks relating to the master plan. Mija had taken a view of the overall plan as well as creating a more detailed level for all the test cycles she would be managing.

'And the coding is scheduled to complete six weeks from now?'

'Yes, according to the plan it is. In reality, though, while the official completion date is in six weeks, Beldor have built in two weeks of contingency.'

'I think that's something we will have to look at. While I'm in favour of inbuilt transparent contingency, I think it should be centrally managed and called out as such. The dates that everyone should be aiming for should be those before contingency is taken into consideration and if there is a delay we should decide in the working groups how we use the contingency. In this case two weeks' contingency is about fifty per cent of the development time, based on a six-week coding period. I know there is some law somewhere that will see that used if it is available.'

Colin looked at Mija with his eyebrows raised. Even though he had been through the plan on numerous occasions with the vendors, had questioned the six-week coding timeframe and was part of the collective sign-off of the baseline, this was the first time he had heard that there was fifty per cent contingency baked in to the schedule.

'I will leave that to you', Mija continued. 'I get most involved once that piece is done. From there we move into the systems integration testing for four weeks and then user acceptance testing for a final four weeks before going live.'

'Do we have the right environments to get this done?'

Mija smiled and took a large format transparent plastic sheet printed with various colourful symbols and overlaid it on top of the Gantt chart.

'This shows the environments we will need in each of the cycles in the front office, operations processing and settlements. We have them booked for the required times and have scheduled a week of availability before testing commences to get the environments ready for the data needed. The names you see here are the specific environment managers who will be responsible for the day-to-day running of the environments to ensure we lose little or no time to unavailability.'

'Then will you be the single point of contact for the testers so that they will not have to contact each of these environment managers if there is an issue with the environment?'

'Yes and no. I will be centrally responsible, but all queries, issues, access requests and privilege management will go through the central testing tool query manager which is linked to a central email address and mailbox. As the testing will be global I will have a regional lead who will be responsible for managing the mailboxes in their time zone and responding to problems raised. These will be logged and tracked to resolution in the testing tool and I will have a review with my team at the start and end of the Belgian day to overlap with Singapore and New York. So yes, I will be managing it as your single point of contact, but I will have regional teams to support me in their time zones.'

'What about instances where it's the interface between two environments where the problem lies?'

'Again, it will be the regional representative who will have contacts for the environment managers and they will coordinate the response.'

'Okay, all of that sounds pretty organised', said Colin, looking at the board. Mija seemed to have it all in hand, but he wanted to ensure that sufficient preparation was in place and that he knew the details intimately. When it came to the testing phases where a test lead was engaged, he could quickly lose control unless he was involved all the way through. Stepping back and assuming it was all in hand meant missing details like the fifty per cent contingency that had been built into the development plan.

'What is this other development item here that seems to be happening during the testing?'

'That's my test team in Poland. Besides writing the test cases and executing the bulk of the testing they will also be writing scripts that will automate the execution of the test cases that they will initially run manually on the new system. They cannot do this until the environment is released for testing. It is more automated scripting than production coding, but we're splitting hairs.'

'Understood. Just so we're both on the same page, can you outline the process end to end so I can align it to what I would expect?' asked Colin, though he expected, having seen Mija's attention to detail, that he would get a fairly textbook response.

'Beldor consultants are writing and refining the business requirements documents aligning them to the target operating model. PolDev are writing the functional specifications based on the business requirements. My team in Wrocław will write the test cases in the online testing tool based on the functional specifications. Each test case will have traceability to the functional specification and from there to the business requirement from which it was originally defined. We expect, based on the requirements written so far, that we will end up with about three thousand test cases. First the technical team will execute these test cases during unit testing, where the test case is modular-specific, and during systems integration testing, where the test cases are end to end. This testing will all be done on the IT-managed development and systems integration testing environments. Once the systems integration testing is signed off, my team in Wrocław will execute the test cases on the user acceptance testing environment. If the test case passes it will be marked as passed in the test tool and then the steps to execute the test case successfully will be scripted so that it can be automatically re-run at the push of a button or as part of a batch job of regression test scripts. If the test case fails, an issue will be raised linking the error back to the test case …'

Colin interrupted and continued, '… which is linked back to the functional requirements, which are linked back to the business requirements, which is linked back to the target operating model.'

'Hey, I thought you wanted *my* take on this?' Mija said, smiling. 'And also to any issue found or comment made when the test case was run in another earlier test cycle or in unit testing or systems integration testing.'

'Don't you think it is risky that *user* acceptance testing is run by an independent team of *non*-users?'

'You must still be jetlagged; we discussed this', said Mija good-humouredly. 'Ten per cent of all test cases will be re-run regionally. This will keep my team honest but will also then take account of any regional differences in booking models and data. If there is no variation found in the results we will stick to the ten per cent, but if we find discrepancies we may need to increase the sample.'

'Has the operations team got capacity to do more than ten per cent?'

'We haven't discussed that.'

'No disrespect to your team in Poland, but I think it would be worth the overlap to start at a higher rate and drop it down thereafter if we find we have no issues than start with a smaller number and increase it if we run into problems. At least then we would capture more problems earlier in the cycle rather than later, when there is less we can do about it while keeping our dates.'

'It makes sense to me, but you may have more difficulty convincing Marcel and Jon, considering that they were particularly pleased at the reduced disruption to their BAU teams.'

'I think it's something they'll have to live with. Besides, I believe that UAT is also the most effective training that any user can have. As broad a section of the end users as possible should be involved so that once the system goes live they will be familiar with it.'

Mija turned back to the board. 'Isn't that all covered as part of the formal training here?'

'The problem with that is the amount of hands-on experience the users in these training courses get. It's only through using it in anger that people get real experience and without this I have seen chaos at go-live. I also believe that while theoretically a complete set of test cases will capture all issues, it is often the peripheral things found during testing that shake out the real problems in the system. Unless the ultimate end users do a significant proportion of the testing we're not going to shake these out.'

'Again, one I will have to leave to you to discuss.'

Colin had been in the office less than an afternoon; he had no connection to the internet and no telephone, yet he already felt particularly productive. To have had the earlier meeting on the phone would have been a completely different experience; and talking to Mija it was obvious that so much of what was taken for granted needed to be revised.

'I don't mind that, I think we can sell it to them easily enough.'

'We'll see', she said. 'I think Jon and Marcel were hoping to cover most of the shake-out you were talking about in production parallel.'

'Excuse me?' asked Colin. 'I'm not sure I heard correctly. Did you say during the production parallel?'

Mija screwed up her face as if she had just stepped into an unpleasant mess left behind by a large farm animal. 'Eh, yes, I know we discussed this before …'

'Yes', interrupted Colin, 'we discussed it before and agreed that a planned production parallel is nothing more than an excuse to run a shoddy UAT. It was not just you and I who agreed; it was also agreed with each of the sponsors at the last plan walkthrough.'

'I do remember that, but even at that time, once the call was done there was a discussion that lasted at least thirty minutes after the call ended where Marcel and Jon agreed between them that they would require a production parallel.'

Colin was realising more and more that he was getting nothing more than lip service when he was at the other end of the phone. He had noticed before, on smaller matters, but with a consistent pattern none the less, that the morning following a conference call, before he had had a chance to write up and distribute the minutes, he would get an email to say that subsequent to the call further discussion with the relevant stakeholders had taken place and a new agreement had been reached. That was when he was informed. It was obvious that he was only seeing the tip of the iceberg.

'And how long is this production parallel supposed to last? It's currently not in any plan I've seen.'

'Well, they don't exactly know, they …'

'That is why I hate the whole concept: it's completely open-ended, it has a beginning but no scheduled end in sight. Usually it will be built around the users being "comfortable" or the system stabilising. All of which are criteria that are completely subjective. It could be done in a week or it could take six months.'

'Don't shoot the messenger, Colin; obviously you have a strong opinion on this, but you may want to choose your fights carefully on this one. They are pretty adamant, and Helena has made comforting noises, if not explicitly agreed.'

'Thanks, but I've been here before. If it's the sponsor's wish that we do this we need to be objective, outline the costs per day of the exercise and try to put in place some objective criteria that everybody can accept.'

'I am taking it that that is easier said than done?'

'In the short term it's quite easy, or it will be with this group of stakeholders. They will be happy to have agreement at this stage of planning that there will be a production parallel in the first place, but rest assured, if the criteria are met and they are still not comfortable then they will change the criteria. It's understandable. I would do the same, and sometimes the risks of getting it wrong are too great. We just need to be there at this side giving a healthy challenge so that we get to the right place in the end.'

'It sounds like you have experienced this before. How do you see the agreement around the production parallel working out? I'd be happy to document it so that we could at least have the discussion around a documented plan and exit criteria.'

Colin looked at the board, thinking. He remembered being in a similar situation before and knew it was important to establish the exit criteria up front; later in the cycle there would be too much noise relating to why the users were uncomfortable and the conversation could not be had at the right level.

'First of all, a production parallel for operations is a dangerous thing to ask for, and I'm not sure how much they've thought it through, especially considering that both Jon and Marcel are so precious about their users getting involved in the UAT. A full production parallel essentially means that all collateral processing will be run in the legacy system and the new system simultaneously at go-live. This will mean that the production teams will have to do everything in the new system that is currently being done in the old system. In addition to this they will need to test the numbers of each system reconcile. Where they are not expected to reconcile due to enhancements and features in the new system they will need to tie back differences to these new features and enhancements and rule out all other possibilities for these differences. This would need to be done every day of the parallel run. If the new system is not kept in sync, the go-live would have to be aborted, the systems cleared down and the exercise started again.'

'But if the production teams do everything in the new system that they do in the old system, wouldn't that mean that the clients will receive two sets of information?'

'That is the one thing that would be turned off on the new system – the interaction with the end client. On this basis it should be transparent to the client. Considering that a full production parallel can double the work for production teams, it is usual to do the parallel run for a subset of clients only. This reduces the parallel processing. The more clients in parallel, the more shakeout of the system can happen, but also the more work needs to be done simultaneously. It is therefore a balance of complete comfort against what can be handled by the operations team. I would start with ten clients in parallel on the new system and set the criteria for cutover to full production processing of these clients as two full days of processing with no new issues greater than high priority. If we stick with this two days, then it is up to the business to specify the add-on clients, understanding what this means for their teams.'

'I'm not sure I follow.'

'Let's say we decide to have ten clients in production parallel and specify two consecutive clean days as our exit criteria. In this case we start at zero days; a day later, if we have no issues, we are at day one complete. If we have an issue we are back to day zero. Once two days have passed with no high-priority issues we are deemed to have met the exit criteria for the ten clients. If the sponsors are still not comfortable they need to add another ten clients to the parallel processing and the two days start again. In this way we don't get to ten days of clean processing of ten clients where the sponsors are not able to make the call to go-live fully for subjective reasons. It really is a no-pain, no-gain scenario.'

'I've never been part of a production parallel like that before.'

'Why would you have been? Your background and expertise is in test management. Scheduling a production parallel is like admitting defeat from the start. If tests were perfect in every way imaginable and unimaginable there would be no need for a production parallel. It is, however, no reflection on you that the theory of testing and the practice are seldom the same and users sometimes insist on a production parallel to account for the imperfections of testing. Though it seems counter-intuitive for a project manager not to plan for the inevitable, I find having production parallel in the plan up front takes the pressure off the users in the test cycles to find everything, as they feel that there is always time in production parallel to fix any issue found.'

'The problem is that it is more expensive to do it that way as the issues are found later and impact the critical path, whereas if they are found earlier they are deployed in the user acceptance testing deployments.'

'True', agreed Colin, 'and besides this they need to go through a standard, longer production deployment as the system will already be technically live. Okay, enough of production parallel; as you get by now it's one of my pet hates. Have we agreed the toll gates with IT deployment for each of the test cycles?'

'Yes, the exit criteria for each cycle is zero blocker issues and critical issues and no more than five per cent of high issues created left open.'

'So by that definition the worse the code the more tolerance we have for open issues?'

'Sorry, Colin, I don't get you.'

'Well, if we find twenty high issues we are willing to allow one issue through to the next round, but if we find twenty thousand we are quite happy allowing a thousand through. I'm sorry if I sound facetious, but that seems to be how the logic works.'

'What would you suggest?'

'How about five per cent of the test cases failing due to high issues?'

'Sure, we can make the change.'

'Are we making a call on open medium and low cases at this stage?'

'We hadn't done, but we could use the same logic and say we would allow ten per cent of the test cases failing due to medium or low issues.'

'Sounds good for a start, though I know from experience we'll bend on that one.'

Colin looked at the Gantt chart and thought about the gate in the photograph again. It was 29 March 2010. He had been here before at this time, under the same conditions, and the chart looked only slightly better at that time. He closed his eyes and took a photo.

13

Test Management

Once again he took his seat opposite the picture of the rusty gate, noticing how he had not thought of it once in the last ten weeks since that initial steering committee on his first day in the Brussels office. He had had hardly any time to help Clara search for a place to live or settle into a new country, not to mind think of a gate in a field. He had not felt too artistic or philosophical in the last ten weeks. He had been consumed by the project.

The last steering committee had not gone well; that was two in a row. As the stakeholders arrived now, he knew it would be a hat trick. The last STC had gone ahead as planned on April 26. It had been held in another part of the building, considered more modern than the client area. 'Modern' seemed to mean that the walls were made of unpainted treated concrete and the art was red. While he did not feel much like artistic interpretation in this meeting, back then he had felt that the walls were closing in like a prison cell and blood was beginning to spill. It had started innocuously enough with the minutes and actions of the last meeting. The business case was presented again and revalidated. This was purely an exercise in going through the motions as it had been covered in individual stakeholder meetings in the run-up to the STC and Jon had already been resigned to leave it in the past by the end of the first STC. On this basis it had been read, agreed, approved and closed.

Things began to become more interesting during the discussion on details of the test plans for systems integration testing, user acceptance testing and go-live cutover. There was no area that did not arouse suspicion or controversy, and for each item a different stakeholder seemed to lead the charge, as if everyone was infected by the red paintings.

'I cannot understand why systems integration testing should take four weeks when we have tested most of the code base ad infinitum in previous incarnations', Marcel stated. 'We have also had a prolonged coding and unit testing cycle. This project is simply adding time and cost for the sake of it. As stakeholders we were not informed how much contingency we had in the coding and then we find out accidentally in an offline conversation that we had fifty per cent contingency built in. A full two weeks! I heard IndoSign were bad, but this I could not believe.'

Colin had in fact sent a note along with the minutes the day after the first STC outlining the contingency that had been included and stating his intention to bring the timelines back by two weeks. The email was, it turned out, filed away unread. It was only when Colin formally raised a request to use one week of contingency due to a slippage in development that Jon flew off the handle. Rather than see it as news that the code would be completed a week earlier than envisaged, he felt deceived and slighted. The STC agreed, against Colin's advice, to cut the final clean-run regression cycle of SIT to shorten it to three weeks. On 21 May both business sponsors allowed the SIT to be signed off by IT with twenty per cent of test cases failing due to medium- or low-priority issues.

'I'm not bothered by the colour of the screen', Marcel had said dismissively about the open lower-priority issues.

There had been some difficult conversations in which priority had been viewed as in some way more subjective, and though Colin had tried to adjudicate as best he could, he felt that the operations and front office stakeholders were being walked all over by Beldor, who were articulate and confident in their more biased assessment. Colin had raised this with Helena, but she had decided not to challenge the business on their view of what was and was not important to them. It was a one-line response to a more thorough and thoughtful compilation of what Colin saw as the problems. It was as if she had suddenly lost interest. Though all blocker, critical and high issues were either deprioritised or had fixes applied, the last batch of ten or so, where code fixes were deployed, were then migrated directly to the UAT environment before a regression test was made across the system. Colin was very uncomfortable that the exit criteria were being breached but was stonewalled by both sponsors. Colin had thought that he would have had more assistance from Helena, but though he was physically closer to her in Brussels it seemed more and more that she was mentally unavailable. It took days for her to answer emails, whereas before it was as if she lived at her email inbox, responding to emails like teenagers do to text messages. His weekly meetings with her had been changed to every other week, and she began to miss these with such regularity that he had met with her just twice in the last ten weeks. She had not even turned up to that last steering committee, when he had had to handle a barrage from all sides.

'Asking the users to execute testing in the first week of user acceptance testing is ludicrous', Jon stated, as if it was the most obvious thing in the world. 'We are paying for an eight-person team in Poland to shake it out before we use it. In this way we will not have to deal with the inevitable teething issues.'

As hard as Colin tried to explain the value of actual users testing the system at this stage, and the added advantage of users getting their hands dirty during the first week (even if the system wasn't perfectly stable), his advice fell on deaf ears. The more he tried to fight one logic with another, the more Jon hardened his stance. Marcel was silent, though Colin could see he disagreed, and Helena was nowhere near to provide support.

That was five weeks ago, and once again he was staring at a rusty gate that somehow seemed rustier than before. Though he told himself that he had no interest in the picture he couldn't help think of Oscar Wilde's *Picture of Dorian Gray*. Things worked out in the five weeks following the last STC broadly as he had expected. He took no pleasure in this knowledge, especially as the project stakeholders drew no parallels, at least openly, between the decisions that they pushed through against his advice and the outcome that followed.

'You have some explaining to do', Jon said as he sat down at the mahogany table on the opposite side to Colin and right at the other end of the table. He was addressing Jörg, who sat on Colin's side and directly opposite Jon.

The political dynamic continued as Marcel arrived and sat next to Jon. Stefan Jacobs, the IT PM, sat one place away from Colin on his left; Mija sat directly next to him on his right, and the chair on his left, where he would have wished Helena to be, was empty.

'Thanks, everybody, for making the time today for this steering committee. As you know, we are at a pretty important stage of the project now that we are two weeks into the user acceptance testing. I have prepared a pack that can walk us through the status of the testing so far and where we will need some form of remediation going forward.'

Marcel was staring at Colin, passive and almost catatonic, while Jon had his head in his hands, possibly reading the actions page under his nose. Colin could see a long vein that ran from his temple along his almost polished crown and it seemed to be throbbing.

'If I could first take you to slide two, which covers the actions since the last meeting.'

'Colin, let's not', Jon replied. 'With all due respect to governance and process I think that we should spend the short time we have together talking about the situation in which we find ourselves in user acceptance testing and what we can do about it.'

His tone sounded as though he wanted to be constructive. Colin knew he wanted to avoid the actions from the last meeting, which in his view were what had brought the project to this point of crisis in the first place. He would look later at this as an offer of a deal to be more constructive if Colin could just move on. He knew logically and practically he should have left it. It could serve no purpose to rile Jon again, he knew how disruptive he could be, but somehow Colin's emotions were playing tricks with the minute decision-making process in his brain. In the milliseconds of indecision, decision and revision he was convinced that to understand how to get from the place they were, they all needed to acknowledge and understand the path that they had taken to get there. He would kick himself later, knowing that his ego had wanted to say 'I told you so', and that raking up the past was better left to a more pragmatic 'lessons learned' exercise where such lessons could be precisely worded both to capture the mistakes and to save the sensitive blushes of the protagonists.

'I think it might be worth, Jon, considering the input the users may have been able to provide in the initial stages of testing.'

'You're completely missing the point, Colin. The code is rubbish. Seventeen weeks ago, long before I even took sponsorship of the project, you took the grandstand in front of my peers telling them all that was wrong in the project, telling them how the code, the vendor, the requirements, the design and so on and so on were all rubbish and had to be changed. Your assertions went as far as the sponsor himself, I've been told, and here we are seventeen weeks later – seventeen weeks later, I will say again – in exactly the same position.'

Colin had regretted his words even as they passed his lips. The first week of testing had seemed to go really well. There were few issues found in testing and the test team, who had access to the environment through systems integration testing and were by now proficient users of both the collateral system and the integrated test management system, were flying through the test cases. The problems began the Monday the end users were let loose on the system. They spent the first day raising issues that were not issues at all but rather related to their understanding of how the system worked. Because they were not used to the integrated test system they took twice as long to raise an issue as it did to execute a test case. Testing was incredibly slow and as they spent more time logging issues than using the system, the perception of system quality was very low, to say the least. By the third day of testing the users were raising issues faster than Beldor and PolDev were able to find answers. By Friday they had raised more than a hundred problems with the system and had insisted that all items were critical or blocker issues. Initial review indicated that the users had continued to raise non-issues, but faster than they could be corrected, and some real issues had been found that would require the focus of the team. The problem was the noise due to everything else that was going on. Colin kicked himself again for dousing the flames with diesel. He needed to turn the conversation back around.

'On the positive side, we now have the ability to trace all open issues back to clearly documented test cases and back to the original requirements. We can also be sure that the fundamental design of the system is in line with the target operating model', Colin began, speaking steadily but continuously, leaving no gap for interruption. He was watching Jon, who looked like a cobra, swaying slightly, poised and ready to strike. 'As you say, however, we have to acknowledge the rocky start we have had to user testing that perhaps the project team could have done more to avoid.' Jon sat back and looked ready to revert to the original deal, seeming to communicate silently that he would give Colin a last chance if he got back in his box. 'What we need now, I hope you will agree, Jon, is to resolve the issues that have been raised and bring more focus to turning answers around more quickly so that there can be more transparency.'

'I think all of that sounds logical in theory. How will you do it in practice?'

'With your support I would like to initiate a war room.'

'A what?' Jon almost guffawed.

'It just means bringing everyone together in one room for the period of the testing so there can be complete focus on getting things done. In practice this means a physical room with the vendor lead, IT PM, subject matter experts, regional lead and myself.'

'What, you lock yourselves in a room until this gets done?'

'That's more or less how it works. We start every day with a formal meeting and go through every issue, triaging it for severity and assigning it to a team for investigation or resolution. For discussions we ensure that everyone necessary is in the room. There are no actions to go and discuss something with someone else and come back to the group. If someone else is needed to resolve a problem, that person joins the people in the war room to discuss the problem and hammer it out. Each issue will be tracked for different states so we know exactly who has responsibility for moving it to the next stage. The war room becomes like a factory for servicing problems. They come through the door, work their way through the different stages, like a production line, and disappear at the end of the line.'

'That all sounds like the most efficient way to work through the problems, even if it is at the extreme end of the scale, but then I like extreme. Why did you say that you specifically need my support for this?'

'I'll need your support, and Marcel's, because I need an hour of your time in the morning and in the evening and I need your SMEs to spend the next two weeks full time testing and taking part in the war room. After two weeks we can take stock of where we are.'

'If that's what it takes, then okay. This has got to be it, though. If you come back in two weeks and say you need to build a cave or something, we're done. I'll make sure my people are completely engaged. Marcel, are you on board?'

'Yes, this should be fine', Marcel replied and while Colin heard the words he hadn't seen his lips move.

'Okay, are we done here?' Jon asked rhetorically, looking around the table for any dissidents before getting up and leaving.

Colin was about to say something. They had not covered any of the steering group pack, which had the status report, issues and risks log and areas for management attention. He bit his lip. The user acceptance testing was the only show in town.

14

Crisis Management in Critical Project Phases

Within an hour the team had occupied one of the project areas with a permanence that could have given them squatters' rights. It was probably the most fit-for-purpose war room Colin had ever had. There were huge whiteboards, a large cinema-size screen and enough wall space to wallpaper with the mountain of coloured Post-it notes he had procured from the stationery cabinet. Stefan, the IT PM, played to his strengths and hooked everyone up to a router he had sourced so everyone could connect to the network and four individual phones. The starfish phone was dialled into a permanent conference line that any of the team could access at any time. The Polish testers were also co-located in a room in Wrocław and permanently dialled into the conference line.

Colin looked around at everyone getting set up. Besides Colin, the permanent war room members included Mija as test lead, Stefan as IT PM, and Jörg to represent Beldor and the development team. Stefanie Burkhart, who was the lead Belgian subject matter expert and who had not been involved with the project team, also joined permanently. Suria Sharma was dialled in from Singapore to act as lead business analyst and had agreed to work central European hours for the two weeks of testing. Suria was joined by Patricia Ng, who would support him with her subject matter expertise. Stefanie was pretty wary of the rest of the team, as project work was pretty different from what she did every day, and she was not really even sure what value it added. Marcel had drafted her in because she knew more about their processes than anyone else in the team. She would be backfilled for two weeks so that she could focus on testing the system and participating in the war room. Looking around the room, she was not sure she was going to fit in very well.

'What's with the colourful paper?' Stefanie asked, even before introducing herself.

'Perfect timing', replied Colin. 'Welcome, everybody. I know some of you have not experienced this type of working arrangement before and I warn you in advance that it can be a memorable experience. For the next two weeks we will live in each other's hair, get on each other's nerves and some-times get so caught up in what we are doing that it will feel like we're at each other's throats. Whatever happens, the next two weeks will be memorable.'

Looking around the room, Colin felt somehow that he had everyone's attention and commitment. Though he could see some had not fully bought into the idea of the war room, everyone was committed to it, as they knew they would either succeed or fail as a result.

'Everything revolves around getting focus on the areas that need to be resolved in the testing environment. Focus itself needs to be prioritised. While a high issue is impor-tant to resolve, and we must resolve it, we need to resolve a blocker first so that other things can be tested while we go after the high items. And not all blocker issues are the same. A blocker that is in unit testing before it is migrated to the UAT environment does not have the same priority as a blocker with no known solution yet.'

'What's a blocker?' Stefanie interrupted. She'd spent the last week testing, and it was one of the field names in the issues log, but she didn't really know what it meant.

'A blocker', replied Mija, glad of the opportunity to educate Stefanie on some testing parlance, 'is an issue that has been identified that blocks other test cases from being executed. For example, if you could not log into the system no other test cases could be executed. This would be an ultimate blocker.'

Stefanie felt that Mija, who seemed smug as could be, was talking down to her. She wondered if it was the time to let the group know that this was the first time she had heard the definition and that no other tester was aware of it either. She had assumed, as other testers probably had, that a blocker was just an issue, an issue that blocked the test case from being completed successfully. She thought that it was probably Mija's responsibility to have instructed them in the first place. They had flown blind initially with the test tracker as it was assumed that they had all used it before and could log issues.

'So', continued Colin, 'to get control of the situation we need to identify, categorise and know every item inside out. Hence the colourful bits of paper, Stefanie.'

'Ah, so we are going to make an issue collage?'

'Great, Stefanie, we'll need humour, and I do hope it lasts. What we are going to do is put every issue we have on the walls and create a production line. The entry point is here.' Colin pointed to the wall and then stuck an A4 sheet of paper on the wall, labelling it 'Open'. 'All new issues and issues that have not moved will be put into this category. Shocking pink notes are for the blockers, orange for the critical and yellow for the high items. We are not going to even bother with the medium and low for now.'

Colin connected his laptop to the large screen and showed a spreadsheet with a download of all the issues. He filtered by blocker issues, reached across for a pink sticky note, wrote a large '17' on the piece of paper and the date it was opened and stuck it under the 'Open' sign.

'The first blocker issue on the list is number seventeen. It goes on the wall under "Open" as there is no fix available for it yet. Not all of these are open, so we need some categories along the wall in line with the progress that has been made.'

Colin made signs for 'In Dev', 'Ready for UAT' and 'Closed'.

'These are the basic categories. I always start with these and somehow we always end up with about ten for different in-between stages, re-opens, and others, but the simpler we can keep it, the better.'

'Shouldn't one of the basic headings be "Rejected"? Looking at the list, we're going to have plenty of these', asked Jörg, already putting his defensive stake in the ground.

'Yes and what about "Duplicate"? I've seen a few of those already too', said Stefan, supporting Jörg.

Colin noticed for the first time that the battle lines were already drawn around the table. Jörg and Stefan were sitting beside each other, Mija had come and sat beside Colin, and Stefanie had not even sat down yet.

'As I said, the list does always get expanded somehow. For me both of those categories fall into "Closed" as they hold no interest for us once they're moved. If it makes you feel more comfortable, though, add the titles next to "Closed" so we keep all the uninteresting items at the end of the production line together.'

'Why don't you just use the spreadsheet?' Stefanie asked. 'I'm being serious this time. All of the issues are in the central testing tool, you download them to the spreadsheet and we track them there.'

'The point of the wall is simply visualisation and familiarity. Within a day we'll know the issues on the wall so well that we won't even need to look at the descriptions in the spreadsheet: all anyone will need to say is a number and you'll remember what the issue is about, where it is on the wall and what colour the piece of paper is. In other words, the priority and what progress it has made. We will continue to be disciplined in updating the central test system and the issue owner will be responsible for each item. When we have our meetings we'll take a cut from the central test system in spreadsheet form as this will continue to be the master copy.'

For the next thirty minutes everyone had a marker in hand and was writing numbers on colourful pieces of paper. Mija had suggested splitting the work between the members of the team. Each person took a category and a severity within the category and updated the wall with the appropriately coloured sticky paper in the correct area. Those who finished earlier moved on to another area that was not being covered. Colin had started with 'Open Blockers', so he continued with this, Stefan took 'Open Critical', Mija 'Open High' and Stefanie 'In Development' blocker items. The team worked through them until everything was done. Now and then, they became side-tracked by discussions on the issues themselves.

'How can this be considered a blocker?' Jörg asked. 'I mean, the issue states that the contrast between the shade of blue on the screen and the text is not high enough. Are you kidding?'

'Just get it on the wall', Colin answered. 'Don't worry, we won't leave today until we're all happy that the wall, and the central test system, Stefanie, reflects our common understanding.'

By the time they were done the room had been transformed from bland and clean to a rainbow of colours. It seemed to vibrate with colour and almost to come alive. The physical representation of the problem was satisfying in itself. The fact that the room glowed shocking pink because the majority of the issues fell into the 'blocker' category was worrying in itself, but the fact that the room was pretty lopsided towards 'open' gave greater concern.

'The test tracking system defaults to "Blocker"', Stefanie said with a smile.

'Good one', said Colin. 'We are going to need to go through these one by one.'

'Colin, I'm being serious. Just because I cracked a small joke earlier doesn't mean that I do nothing but joke around. I have been testing all through the week and raising issues. The test system defaults to "Blocker" and, what's more, the meaning of the word was never explained to any of the testers. The dropdown is probably ordered alphabetically with blocker as the first item and leaving it as the default means one less item to change when opening an issue. I have left the default there myself thinking that blocker meant a test case that blocked successful execution. If I am guilty of leaving as the default, my guess is that the other users are also just not changing it.'

'We can change the default to blank; it's not difficult', Mija suggested.

'Already done', came a voice from over the speakerphone, making half the room jump; they had all forgotten that Poland and Singapore were permanently dialled into the conference call.

'Okay. My apologies, Stefanie, and thanks for the suggestion. We will also need to inform the users of the meaning of the criteria. Mija, could you please send an email to all users explaining the clinical definitions of Blocker, Critical, High, Medium and Low? We also need to ensure that they are using the objective descriptions and not what they could mean subjectively. Hopefully new issues will begin to have something more sensible from tomorrow and we can agree on priority for those open today.'

The conference line beeped twice and the voice of Serge Baranov announced that he had joined; at the same time Jon and Marcel walked into the room. Colin had lost track of time in the excitement of setting up the war room and not realised that the first discussion call was due to start. Jon and Marcel were walking around the room looking at the walls.

'Now I see what you mean', Jon said, without turning back from the walls. 'It looks good, and pretty bad if you know what I mean.'

'Thanks for joining', Colin responded. 'I hope it looks worse that it really is.'

For the next two hours they went though every single issue one by one. Where an item needed to be amended, the issue owner updated the online tracking tool and Colin changed the wall by moving the Post-it from 'Open' to 'In Dev' or even directly to 'Closed' where it was agreed that the items raised were non-issues. Where issues' priority was changed they were rewritten on a new coloured sticky note. Some issues were found to be lower priority than they had agreed to track in the war room and these were moved to a new category called 'Deferred'. By the time they had gone through every item the wall looked significantly more manageable, with just five pink Post-its remaining in the 'Open' category, where they were joined by ten orange and six yellow. Colin felt somehow the team was boosted to see the progress before their eyes. All eyes stayed on the wall.

'What a beautiful collage', said Stefanie.

'My kind of art', replied Colin.

15

Delivery

Colin found himself staring past the bar to the illuminated photograph of a field of long grass with long-stemmed red flowers in the foreground. The last three weeks had drained him completely. The war room was as intense as any in which he had participated or run before. Every day was different, with new issues to deal with and constant dynamic planning. The team took three days to get behind the idea that everyone had the same objective, to get the system live with code quality and functionality that everyone could support. For some reason Mija and Stefanie also seemed to rub each other up the wrong way. It was textbook forming and storming of team management. Colin was relieved that by the third day the team was understanding and following the process – or norming. Though the team performed what it needed to do, the intensity of the task meant that it was never a calm, collegial team environment.

'The major problem we are going to have in getting this over the line is the throughput of test cases by the users', Mija had begun. 'We have fifteen hundred test cases left to complete and now only eight business days remaining. With four users that means about fifty test cases per day per user and we only got ten each done yesterday.'

'Mija, you are forgetting that we lost four hours due to batch re-runs and it just so happened that this was at the quietest part of the day for the collateral processing team, so they could have done much more. It doesn't help either that for every three test cases they execute they need to raise an issue against one of them.'

'Stefanie, the highest throughput of any user to date has been twenty-seven test cases by, let me see, Marcus Dubois. You know we can extract these statistics from the test tool. On this basis, if everyone was to do as well as Marcus, it would take us about three weeks to complete, and we know that that's not going to happen overnight. My test team in Wrocław were executing fifty test cases per person in the first week.'

'Yes, we know that, and they passed practically all of the test cases they executed. They didn't even need to spend time raising issues. That was pretty convenient. And look where their speed got us. They are also more familiar with the test system and the test cases – they wrote them, for goodness' sake, and they have had weeks to play around with the system and the testing tool. How you can expect the users to be anywhere as fast is beyond me. Where did you even come up with the estimates for testing? Were they pulled from the air?'

Colin took a sip of his beer. He had a little left in the glass and was waiting to get the attention of the bartender. He still found it strange that there was bar within the Bank IB premises; it felt like he was back in college, where there was a bar on campus. That spat between Stefanie and Mija was one he was pretty careful about getting in the middle of. With only two days of the war room behind him he could not be seen to take sides. He needed both Stefanie and Mija to apply themselves for the duration and actually work together rather than being at each other's throats.

'Look', he interjected, 'it is a fact that if the users continue at the pace they are executing test cases, and if we expect them to execute all test cases, the time will need to be extended. This is no reflection on the users, just a fact of where we are, the experience the users have and the maturity of the code that they are testing. We need to look at what test cases they are executing and see if we can reduce the burden on them. If they are repeating scenarios we should give the repetition with new data to the Wrocław team to manage. We could change the process so every test case is not executed in every region but rather ensure that region-specific test cases are run in the region where they are needed and a cross section of the more generic test cases are shared between teams. We need to look at other ways of doing this rather than revisiting why we got here. There will be ample time for that post go-live when we will need to do a comprehensive "lessons learned" exercise. The Wrocław test team passed some test cases in error in the first week. We have investigated the reasons for this and implemented remediation, so we should have fewer issues on that front. I would still recommend that we have users spot-check some of the executed test cases.'

Both Stefanie and Mija seemed to have taken a step back and drawn a breath. Stefanie had offered to work over the weekend with some of the users to increase the through-put of test cases, and Mija, who had seemed impressed by her commitment, had matched the offer and arranged for environment support to boot. They looked at some of the suggestions put forward by Colin and implemented some of them. Stefanie did not want to reduce the burden of the testers too much as they would have to live with the system once it was live and had already seen the impact of taking shortcuts. On a more positive note, the code itself, once redeployed, was of pretty good quality. There were issues found, but when the error was detected and a fix deployed it usually worked the first time. Working with IndoSign they had been plagued with issues that the developers had fixed that were all reopened when the test case was executed again. By the end of the first week the issues were being tracked through the production line just using the reference number.

'Where are we with one hundred and two?' Mija asked.

'It's there in "QA Passed"', responded Jörg, pointing to the wall where yet another category had been added.

'Let's move it to "Ready for UAT" and ask the users to retest', suggested Stefan.

The conversations had continued like that through the day and at each war room call they focused on the open items that needed to be moved on.

'Why is sixty-seven still in "Open"? I thought we had a solution for this', Colin had asked.

'We agreed the solution, but it is a change request and not an issue. We have no documented business requirements, so we have not begun coding', replied Stefan, who had seemed to come alive in the last days of the war room.

'I'll have it to you in an hour', came the reply from Suria in Singapore.

The last week of testing raised a larger concern. As the users became more confident and were executing above the required number of test cases they went 'off-piste', as Stefanie was fond of calling it. They began testing things that were not within the test scripts and in the process finding bugs or required change requests to the requirements. This was pretty concerning as there was no way to define how long this free-form testing would take. There was no way to measure it by test cases and time limiting it made no business sense either. It became a bit exciting at one point, but even with all users going 'off-piste' the number of bugs dwindled pretty quickly. Of course the production parallel was not avoided and this was part of the agreed remediation for the possibility that there were test scenarios that had not been written. Colin knew that it was unavoidable weeks before the UAT was completed successfully. Successful completion of the UAT was not taken for granted for a moment during the testing phase. Every day there was something new, but as the days went by and the test cases were executed, the input side of the wall became plainer by the day, while the uninteresting area was a meadow of colour. With every move of a piece of paper from one area of the wall to the next the mood had become more optimistic. It was tangible, and even Mija and Stefanie seemed to get along. When the user acceptance testing was signed off, the team were ready to celebrate. Having gone through the war room for two weeks, worked into the night and at weekends, everyone was delighted that it was complete and became visibly upset when Colin had asked for it to continue for the week of parallel run. They understood in the end that it would require one last push to get it over the line and relegate the war room to history.

The migration to production was as smooth as could be and a credit to the IT team and vendors who had managed it flawlessly. The shock came when the first client was put in the parallel environment and it turned out that collateral was calculated differently between the new and legacy systems. Jon went ballistic. Ten clients were added the second day and it was found that the calculations were consistently different. The problem was that no one could find any flaw in the logic of the requirements or the implementation of the requirements. The shock came when Jon and Marcel realised that the legacy system had been using an incorrect calculation for a certain type of trade and collateral had been requested from clients at a reduced rate. At that point Jon switched from cautious to gung-ho and carried Marcel with him. It was the last push that was needed to move from production parallel into full production.

That was only eight hours ago, and finally everyone involved was enjoying a celebratory drink together. While Colin was ordering a round for the team, he continued to stare at the picture behind the bar. The flowers were a vibrant shade of red and everything around them was a lush green.

It was then that he realised that the flowers were growing where the gate had been and he felt eyes stare through him at the picture and turned to see Helena.

'Helena, I guess you heard then?' he asked, somehow not knowing what else to say. Helena had been missing for weeks.

'Of course I did', she said, 'I've been watching your progress very closely.'

'I wasn't sure; it seemed you were not so close over the last few weeks.'

'There was a reason for this.'

'There usually is, it seems.'

'You may not have heard, but Christine Kale has been promoted to head of shared services. The selection process has been ongoing for months now, and parallel to that I was being evaluated to take on Christine's role as head of operations. I found out two weeks ago that it had been agreed. Christine and I have been working on the transition over the last two weeks in advance of the announcement and I've been evaluating a replacement for my role as global head of change.'

'Congratulations, Helena, that's great news', Colin said, though he was concerned that he would be losing a supporter in Helena as she moved on, and he would have to transition to a new manager all over again.

'Colin, it is you I've been evaluating in the last weeks. I needed you to stand on your own against Jon and Marcel. They have also been aware for some time. In truth it was the position I hired you for from the outset and I'm glad it has worked out. That is, of course, assuming that you're up for the challenge?'

Colin didn't know what to say.

'That is one of the series, isn't it?' he asked. 'I mean the series with the rusty gate.'

'That is number one hundred and twenty', she said, raising her glass. 'It's the final one. Congratulations!'